# The Whole Shebang

## Sticky bits of being a woman

# The Whole Shebang
## Sticky bits of being a woman

Lalita Iyer

BLOOMSBURY
NEW DELHI • LONDON • OXFORD • NEW YORK • SYDNEY

First published in India 2017
This export edition published in 2020



ISBN: 978-93-86432-28-5

Bloomsbury Publishing India Pvt. Ltd
Second Floor, LSC Building No. 4
DDA Complex, Pocket C – 6 & 7, Vasant Kunj
New Delhi 110070
www. bloomsbury. com

Typeset by Manipal Digital Systems

# Contents

# Prologue

## This woman business

I am quite sure this book will not tell you much about 'How to be a woman'. I don't know how to write that sort of thing, as I'm still figuring it out. What I do know is that being a woman is a serious amount of admin. I am sure being a human is too, but if you factor in hair management (everywhere, all the time), ovulation management (once a month for most of us), relationship management (all the time, for all of us), parent management (even if you produce half a dozen kids, your parents will still treat you like a child), pregnancy (at least once in a lifetime for some of us), and marriage (hopefully not more than once in a lifetime) – you know what I am talking about.

We are all born with a daughter tag; the rest get added along the way: sister, cousin, friend, girlfriend, wife, mother, daughter-in-law, sister-in-law, ex-wife, boss, subordinate, grandmother, step-mother and whatnot. With every tag comes more admin and more ways of being.

But no matter what you do, the nagging feeling of something left undone is what constitutes being a woman for the most part. Some of us forget to marry, others forget to have kids, a few marry the wrong guy but forget to tell him that, a few walk away but forget to move on; meanwhile our mothers are still figuring out what we do for a living and asking us to comb our hair. And while filing taxes should be on autopilot by now, we still have trouble finding proof of all our investments.

And so there are always checklists crawling beneath our epidermis, reminding us of things left undone. This obviously does nothing to assuage our inadequacies, and the stakes continue to be raised every single day, no matter what we do or don't do.

How does one then get ahead?

Even if you may have wrapped your finger around money, savings, ovulation, fashion and a career you truly belong to, things like hair and love still remain beyond your control. Some of you may have figured out man, marriage, baby, career, home, and a botox and tummy tuck plan. This book is for the rest of you who don't necessarily believe that marriage and babies are the happily ever after for a woman. For those who are still dealing with imperfections and happy to say "I am enough".

We all yearn for just that right blend of purpose, independence, common sense and madness and even when we get there, we are never sure we are there really. Our sense of self, which is quite delicate, tends to get into an insidious loop of fragility with the slightest aberration in our plan. To make matters worse, your legs are never waxed the day you bump into an ex and perhaps that's why you are clad in a tent and can't appear breezy as you intended to.

One would imagine that with one set of parents, siblings, one marriage, one baby, few books and around a dozen jobs and cats behind me, I must be spiffingly together. Not. And this book will not end with how you can get it all together, because in the end, no matter what you do, you really can't.

What it could probably do for you is remind you that it's the same shit everywhere. That thousands, millions of women who you look up to, adore, role model on, have been there, done that and are still figuring it out. Same shit, different place.

The book found its genesis in the columns I wrote over the years, chiefly Chickwit (HT Café), Parentology (Pune Mirror) and Parentitis (Indian Express) and some of my work that appeared in Elle, National Geographic Traveller, Vogue, Elephant Journal, Times Crest and my blog, mommygolightly.com. If you read familiar bits here, there was a germ somewhere in the aforementioned publications.

# 1. How I met my period

In the month of February of my fifteenth year on this planet, while studying in my balcony for my class X board exams (we were granted a three-week study leave), I got my period. Got is what they said in those days, and 'chums' was the popular euphemism.

It was not supposed to be this way. Where was the audience? My parents were at work, my siblings were at school. I was home alone, studying. I mean, who gets their periods studying? The least that could have happened was I could have got it at Bharatanatyam class or during the goddamn assembly while my all-girls school was still on. PT class would have been even better, on account of the white uniform, hence hard to miss stain. I envied the other girls in my class the drama of the stain. The whispering, the discovery, the shock, the denial, the submission, and finally the whisking away and being allowed to go home early on account of a 'medical emergency'.

This of course implied that by some subtle private club code, they were thereby initiated into womanhood. I also felt that the girls in a co-ed school would have been a lot less mean, as they would have to fake solidarity in front of the boys. But in a high-estrogen all-girls convent, all fangs were out at all times. If you hadn't got your period, you didn't count. I didn't, clearly, despite being a top-ranker and all that.

Even the flat-chested front benchers were crossing over to the other side, one by one. All except Annie and I (although she told me she got hers, I knew she was lying). I was close to nervous wreckage. Of course there were tiny eruptions in the name of breasts (and they hurt). And hair was sprouting in places other than my head. So I knew my body was up to something. Yet, there was no visible evidence. The constant barbs about 'gender unknown' by the back-benchers in my class, the constant looking at me in a "Serves you right, you show-offy, always-doing-your-homework-on-time first bencher"! The speaking in code about 'downs' and 'my sister' and 'that time of the month' as if I didn't know what they were talking about. It was as though I was paying a price for my academic excellence. "Let her know what it means to win a consolation prize," the signs seemed to say.

My mother had always been mysterious about 'the period', as though saying the word would start the taps; she never gave me the birds and the bees talk. Neither did my friends, although one neighbour who was eleven and 'chumming' made it a point to tell me all the gory details, in the manner of "well, I got there before you, see!" Being the first-born didn't help at all. So I was left to figuring it all on my own, reading subtext and often reading what was not written.

I had however dragged my mother to buy me a bra and the best they could do at the shop was a 28A, for my chest pimples. Since college life was looming large, I was concerned about being the first girl to go to college without a period (I was already planning on faking it by spilling sanitary napkins every time I took out my wallet, in case the blasted red river never showed up). And the bigger concern was about actually being a man in disguise, although my mother always hushed me when I spoke such unmentionables. I truly needed an assurance that I was ready for bearing children which I never wanted to have. “Give me this day my fertile ovaries” was my prayer.

In the light of all this, the ‘no audience’ thing upon arrival of the red river was a real bummer. I would never get to tell my class girls that I (finally!) got my period. That I *was* them, just a late bloomer is all.

I made a mental note of announcing it to my class when the board results were declared two months later (and I topped, again, and it meant nothing, again), but then girls were just running helter skelter, collecting marksheets, bonafide certificates and rushing to stand in queues for college admissions and whatnot and who would be interested in my period? So my little celebration never really happened with the ones who really mattered.

When my mother came home that afternoon, after I had wallowed sufficiently in my red river and the cramps thereafter (and had run out of fabric wads to stuff my panties with) I announced to her that I was a woman. She said, Thank god. Or something to that effect.

I liked the fact that finally I got to pick a side (I could tick ‘female’ in all boxes now) and could now be officially in on all the sex talk at school.

From that day on, the red river was a loyalist, and I was constantly assured that it would never fail me, always knocking on my door in 28 days exactly. (Years later, my ob-gyn told me that my regular-as-clockwork menstrual cycle was what made conceiving at 40 easy as pie for me. “You are lucky,” he said.)

With periods came period paraphernalia. In my time, you got these Comfit sanitary napkins, whose ads always featured women (or was it a man and a woman?) running in slow motion, hugging trees and suchlike. This was pre-Whisper days, but even then, girls always ran in slow motion during their period. Then came the Carefree era which was Comfit with two long tails and a plastic sheath. This was followed by the revolutionary peel off pads – Stayfree, Whisper and the gang. And what do you know? Very soon, pads had wings. (I am sure this was trying to say something about the women's movement.)

Comfit pads looked like fluffy white sausages with tiny ears. These ears had to be looped with utmost dexterity in between the white and the red plastic loops pre-strung through an elastic ring/band which they proudly called 'the belt'. This was very complicated and involved too much technique, especially in your most vulnerable and therefore clutzy days. My series of unfortunate incidents involving Comfit often featured the plastic loops in the front shooting off just as I wore the band and was ready to get padded and me frantically looking for them in the bathroom when someone had to 'go' really urgently. Sometimes, I just shoved a few sausages into my underwear and couldn't be bothered about the loops and it never really mattered, unless of course, your underwear wasn't well fitted. (But more about period underwear later.)

The tricky bit was finding this belt in that newspaper-wrapped Comfit packet. The belt was usually knotted into a tiny ball and placed delicately amid the bundle of pads and you almost always couldn't find it until you had spilled all the pads on the floor and ruined a few in the process. The pack announced 'free belt inside', but they should have had a contest for finding it in less than five minutes. Once the belt was found and you could go about your business, the tricky part was figuring out how to minimize the lag time between discarding a used pad and adding a new one (no one talks about this either).

And then someone invented the horror called the period panty. And every mother bought one for her daughter. If you remember what it was like to be an infant, to always have your genitals covered and smothered in a diaper (cloth or otherwise) and never be able to come up for air, well, that's how a period panty felt. Every girl must have tried them at least once, because they were advertised as 'stain-proof' and 'secure protection' and 'no more accidents' and everything unsubtle. These were made of two layers – an outer nylon or rayon or whatever material produces the maximum irritation to your skin and an inner – hold your breath – plastic sheath. In case you were a nincompoop who still hadn't learned how to use a pad, there were two elastic bands on the inside of the panty to hold your sanitary pad in place.

'Changing a pad' was some sort of expedition or conquest, with girls constantly exchanging notes on how often they changed. In some circles, not changing often was looked at with awe, in others, with pity, as if secretly passing judgment that the ovaries were perhaps not healthy enough or not doing a good job of getting rid of the unfertilized egg. But whatever the pronouncement, there was always a thrill about knowing that if you had a period, you had just about missed a pregnancy. That you were almost pregnant. For a little girl, that information can be huge.

When I grew up, I realised that there were two kinds of women: those who make a big deal of their period and those who pretend it doesn't exist and look at you in askance when you bring it up. Why did they do that, I wondered. I was veering dangerously to the other side and I didn't know why. Perhaps because I always saw my mother slumped and gloomy during her period and I was determined that I was not going to let mine get in the way of fun.

Balancing your period with the rest of your life was what the rest of your life was going to be. So you had to plan waxing cycles, treks, beach fun, sex, presentations, dates, travels, even your own wedding, around your period.

I was, at the time of onset (of the period of course), a follower of tennis and constantly in awe of Martina Navratilova, Chris

Every Lloyd and Steffi Graf for how they 'managed' their period with their tournaments while my mother had programmed me to be nervous even about a train trip during 'those days'. They were always so poised in their short, white skirts with their underwear showing, and when I asked why I could never see the bulge of the pad ever, my friends whispered, 'tampons'. Like it was some code for big girl talk. My friends also told me they took 'pills' to control the period, but then I wondered how they could take pills all the time? And would that not make their ovaries totally nuts, never knowing when they could gush.

Soon as I managed to shove a tampon into my vagina, I did, because wrapping the pad and walking eternally to the other end of the college/hostel/office was unbearable, what with you feeling that you had been marked and were off to an unexciting expedition. I later learned that girls who wore tampons were marked as 'those' type of girls – the ones who always get a lot of action down there, so their vaginas are like butter to slide the tampons in and out. No one actually compared the size of a tampon to an average penis, but never mind. I found it odd that most girls associated tampons with loss of virginity.

At some stage you reached a point where you could talk to men (at least some of them) freely about your period and they pretended to understand, perhaps having been trained by previous girlfriends or able sisters or mothers. But I still wonder whether they really, truly get it and can feel empathy in this regard. Because unless a man has a period, he has no idea what a woman goes through.

I used to often wonder about period waste and how much it must be contributing to landfills and feeling less guilty that my three decade tampon usage must have contributed far less. Now I hear women talking about how the menstrual cup has set them free. The period revolution is finally here! Can you believe not having to ever change a pad or a tampon, but just inserting this silicon wonder into your vagina, allowing the menstrual blood to drain into it and then just rinsing it and reinserting? I am trying to imagine how much money I may have spent on pads and tampons in the years since my period, and it's scary. That is one math I don't want to do. But I have decided to give the menstrual cup a miss nevertheless. I don't want to shock my uterus at this stage of my life.

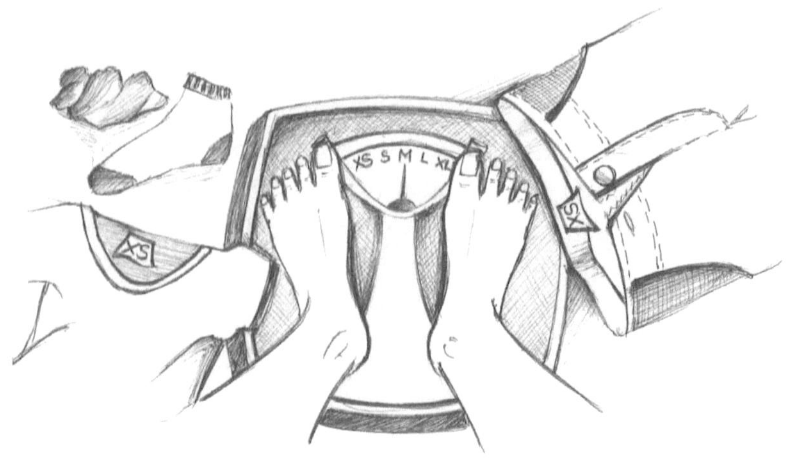


# 2. Body image, size and other tricky things

I have always had the knack of having the right body at the wrong time. When voluptuous was in, I was skinny. When stick insects were in, my breasts runneth over in my 36 C postpartum cups.

I spent the first thirty years of my life thinking I had too little. Too little height. Too little beauty. Too little breasts. Too little mouth. Too much hair.

Then I went through ten years of totally loving my body, my hair, my face and me.

Now I wish I could have some back (from the phase when I thought I had too little).

For the last eight years, post giving birth, I have been pretending my body isn't mine. It is something that exists in an alternate universe – I didn't make it, I certainly didn't earn it, and I unfortunately can't control it. And yet, I keep classifying it into the good bits, the can do with some work bits and the downright ghastly bits.

Every once in a while, I muster the courage to walk into a Mango or Zara or Promod and try on clothes which fit one part of my body but don't fit another and I tell myself – I am totally out of proportion. What I don't tell myself is that these clothes were made to squash me into someone else's shape.

I find that poor body image is just an extreme case of vanity. What else would you call a phenomenon that allows the examination of our body so much and constantly wants it to match up to someone else's standards? Reverse vanity? Our body police range from the media police, insensitive workmates, social media, even family, often rank strangers who don't hesitate to give you advice on your body and what you must do with it.

As a small person (who wore XS until she was 28) I was constantly encountering bigger women. For most of my life, I have been surrounded by women bigger than I, which is not a difficult thing to achieve, as I am five feet nothing and I pretty much stopped growing vertically at age fifteen.

I have always been in awe of big women. There are those who thrust their bigness in your face (read, if you are walking down a corridor and they are walking towards you, you can be sure that if you don't retreat, they will run you over). And there are big women who don't give a damn, and would never try a slimming product or aspire for a certain size or fit … they wear their bigness with aplomb and in fact you actually like them because they are big, and couldn't bear to imagine them any other way.

Then there are those who hate you for being small and secretly wish they could fit into your clothes. Such women go on crash GM diets, dancersize and zumba classes, or pretty much anything that promises to make them svelte. It does, relatively speaking – it helps them lose 3 kg of their total 80 kg body mass, but that hardly shows. So they are usually sore and grimacing most of the time.

And finally, there those who are almost apologetic about being big – they try to physically shrink when they are near you. They have a genial attitude, softer voices, gentler footsteps, and you feel safe and protected around them – almost like baby bear feels around mamma bear.

When I grew up, I wanted to be big. Never medium. Medium was nothing. Medium was neither here nor there. Medium had no personality, no gravitas, no backstory.

32B cups and size 26 jeans were my best friends for years. Size zero still wasn't in yet, so I basked in my glory. I had good limbs, a décolletage when I needed one, my ass was as perky as ever and there was no dearth of sales I went to and the clothes I bought. 'Extra Small', I'd proudly announce even as the sales girl tried to hand me a Small. I was the size to envy. I bought tiny little skirts, boots, ultra short shorts in which I could flaunt my bronze legs, singlets and tank tops that revealed my bone structure. I was the girl who would float in someone else's clothes every time I had a sleepover, and I could never get enough of, "Oh god, how tiny are you?"

A friend of mine told me how she finds it tough being taken seriously by her juniors at work, as they were all bigger than her. "It's about filling a chair ..." she said. "You have to have to appear big to look intimidating." And sometimes, when you have to kick ass, it helps to be bigger than your opponent, so you at least know that they can't punch harder than you. When big people talk, you always find yourself paying attention. I always thought the only way to be was tiny or big, but never in between. I liked big girls. They had so much gravitas. They made you look up, they made you make room for them, they never sucked their stomach in, they looked so cool when they smoked and they could really carry off jewelry.

I tried wearing layers and appearing large, inhaling deeply and filling myself out, outstretched arms and all in an ample chair, but felt like a bit of an idiot. I finally assured myself that it was okay to be small and people will take you seriously one day and that sometimes, great things do come in small packages.

Fortunately or unfortunately, I have never aspired to appear taller or larger by wearing heels or padded bras – I really didn't see any point in creating an illusion.

And then I grew up.

I had moved from thin to voluptuous. It was a shift, but I didn't mind it.

Cut to pregnancy, motherhood, nursing and more breast action. I added on 15 kilos and dropped them in the next six months post-delivery. The breasts stayed, but I was back in my size 28 jeans. What post-baby body were they talking about?

May be it was voodoo, but three years post-baby, I was somehow something of a blob. When I last checked, my rib cage, waist and hips were the same dimension as each other. I am square. I'm Rani Mukherji, I thought. It was official. I had moved from XS to S to M.

This is it, I thought. This is the beginning of the end. I am Medium. I am nothing.

I stopped buying anything that had a waist (including jeans) because I didn't have one anymore. Empire line dresses and leggings never said no, no matter how much I grew. I passionately embraced them. Maxis were the new me.

And then I found saris. I always loved their drape and how they could do as much or as little as you wanted. I had quite a few that I had stacked up in a trunk (in my youthful body phase that was all about flaunting limbs, the poor sari had taken a backseat). There they were, inviting me to start all over again.

I found new joy in blouses. Funky, psychedelic, elegant, elaborate – I bought any fabric I liked and imagined it as a blouse.

Sometimes I mixed them up and gave them totally new identities. I serial-dated tailors till I found the right guy. It never bothered me when a blouse didn't have a sari to flirt with. If the blouse rocks, the sari will find its way, I thought. And it did. Friends were suddenly gifting me saris, I became a hand-me-down mascot. Each time I visited my mother, an old sari beckoned me. My measurements are locked up in a nice little book with my tailor. He doesn't judge me. He never will.

In an age where relationships are as old as Facebook accounts, perhaps no one will now remember that I had a thin past. But thin is not a mother's best friend. Thin is not inclusive. Thin is what people who 'got stuff done' were.

My mother recently told me I've never looked healthier in my life. I read this as: This is the fattest you have ever been. It's a bit depressing to know that your mother thinks you were all wrong for most of your life. But I still smiled.

When men ask me if I've put on weight, I say, "I gave birth. What's your excuse?"

When I go clubbing, I don't think sexy anymore. I think comfy, snug, something in which I don't have to fidget too much, fabric that flaunts the nice bits and camouflages the not-so-flattering bits. I still have legs. Although I'm yet to fathom what has happened to the rest of my body. The last time I wore an LBD, my Facebook profile picture got 120 likes. "Hot mamma!" one said. No one noticed that it was very clever dressing. People still want to believe in the idea of thin-me.

I don't have aspirational jeans in my closet waiting to motivate me. If I don't fit into them, someone else will. I have regular hand-me-down dates with women who still have the body for clothes I once had a body for. Surprisingly, it makes me happy to see them in clothes that once fit me so well. I'm also happy to take clothes from big girls who are happy to see their small clothes on me.

Medium is a whole new ecosystem for me. I have gathered enough equanimity to glide over the politics of thin and pretend I have left the room. I have made my peace with my contours or the lack thereof. I have stopped treating my body like a Work in Progress. I might have occasional flings with Spanx, but it will never be someone who can move into my life. Thin is past tense and I'm happy to let it stay that way. The boobs and ass are here to stay, and so are the pelvic wattle and the thick waist.

But the last time I went to a store and wanted to try something, and the lady assistant said, "Wait, this is Large. I will get you Medium," I was grateful. Ever. So. Grateful.

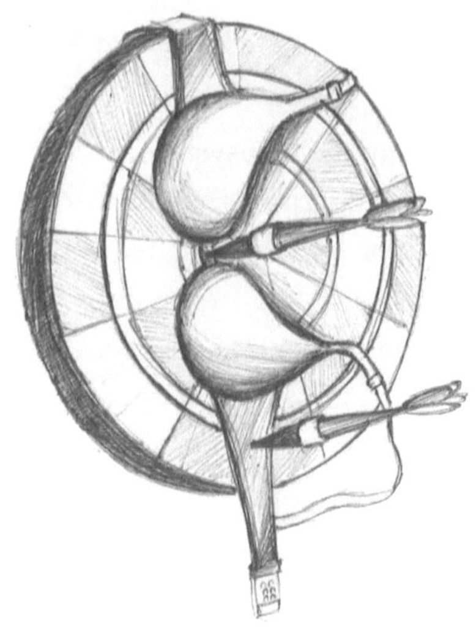

# 3. Underwire and other instruments of womanly torture

Once upon a time, I was 14 and bra-less. With my puny frame and no period around the corner, I was pining for Ms. Puberty, bras (and therefore breasts) and some curves. My consolation prize at the time was that I was the clichéd first bencher: I knew the answers to the teacher's questions in class, I had good handwriting, I aced composition writing.

I thought that would get me the boys.

Wrong.

Since my mother had already done the unpardonable thing of moving me to an all-girls convent school (euphemism for nunnery) in grade 5, boys were not things that you went to school with, played with, shared benches with, or copied homework from. They were now things to be sought, won and conquered; they were no longer a part of your default setting.

One of the chief ingredients that attracted boys to girls, we were told at the time, were breasts. If you had the boobs, you got the boys, they said.

It seemed to be true. Neeta and Shaheen, my two girl crushes and role models in class nine already had boyfriends (boy next door and boy across the street, respectively, who they incidentally married and lived happily ever after with) and continued to raise the bar on displaying their womanhood in class. Neeta wore her bra inside her white pinafore shirt WITHOUT A SLIP. So basically, no veil between the bra and the shirt, which means that everyone in school assembly knew you were wearing a bra!

I mean, that took guts. The slip/chemise, or what my mother called 'shimmy', was an inbetweener that was supposed to camouflage the fact that you had breasts and therefore wore a bra, although I never really saw how that worked. But it was the school's rule that all girls wore slips to cover their modesty (aka bra) and a few like Neeta dared to defy it. Another girl who did it with aplomb was Sandra Evans. She was two years senior, danced Bharatanatyam like a goddess, played throwball like a badass, cussed like the boys and watched adult movies and talked about sex all the time. And she was drop dead gorgeous and had the boys at her beck and call. On non-uniform days, Sandra always wore see-through tops that revealed her bra strap(often black, red and other 'slutty' colors that girls of a certain age didn't wear). If you were close enough to her, you could sometimes see the lace in the front, and very often, she left a few buttons open, so you could take a peek at her cleavage. I told myself, this is what I want to be. If you got it, flaunt it.

When I get breasts, I will also chuck my pathetic 'shimmys' I thought. They were all home-stitched by my mother and had flower motifs or embroidery (also by her), as if that made up for not growing breasts.

I figured wearing a bra was the first step to womanhood, and since the period took its time, I thought I might as well get on with the rest of it. So one day, I pointed at my swellings and told my mother I needed a bra. 28A was the best the bra-shop could do for my nonexistent breasts. I settled, because I had to start somewhere. I was already feeling galaxies away from Sandra-ness.

The bra didn't feel as great as they said it would. For the most part, I was just fidgety: constantly adjusting, pulling it down all the time, as it had a tendency to ride up and suffocate me. Since I was asthmatic, I couldn't tell the difference between an asthma attack and being choked by my own bra. It was always clumsy. It still is, actually, but I seem to have developed a nonchalance about it. And if you are finding my bra predilections a bit overwhelming, wait till I get to the chapter on knickers. Or skip it, if you think it will get your panties in a bunch.

It was as though bras (or brassieres) were the official technical prop for being a woman. You needed them to validate your womanhood, as your breasts grew, you had to find newer, more expensive, more innovative ways to torture them. And it almost felt pointless because every bra was simply waiting to be taken off. Being able to wear underwear (especially bras) intelligently is a talent that women have to hone.

The real breasts took their time, but one day I was a proud 32B. It was time for underwire, I was told. Of giving the breasts their due (read décolletage). It's true, underwire bras made this shit look good; they really gave your breasts that much needed gravitas. Little did I know that it was the most painful gravity-defying decision one could ever make. I don't mind a little padding to round off the edges, but some of these bras make you feel like you were wearing a pillow on each boob!

I can say with a certain amount of certainty that the underwire bra would rate as one of the most medieval instruments of torture. After the initial gloating at one's (newly acquired) cleavage, and the way your shirt fits over it, the way your breasts acquire a mind of their own and sway and heave, you usually do what I do. Fidget. Pull the front, pull the back, adjust the straps, breathe out, breathe in, and just pray that you can get through the day without constantly being aware that you are wearing a bra.

Women who can get by an entire day without fidgeting with their bra – I want to have what you are having. It's been over three decades of bra-wearing and there is not a single day I don't fidget. Or when I don't get told one of the following:

*Maybe you are not wearing the right size.*

*I only wear <insert name of brand that costs an arm here> I never have a problem.*

*You should try seamless. It's so comfortable, you can sleep in it.*

*I buy all my bras when I travel.*

*Have you tried getting yourself measured?*

And then those radio ads from Marks &Spencer have women exclaiming, "Did you know that 80% of women are wearing the wrong *launjerray*?" Yes of course, at the prices they came at, bras suddenly began to be referred to as 'launjerraaaay'.

Yes, I was among the 80% of women ashamed to admit they are wearing the wrong bra, especially after paying 3000 rupees for it and thinking it's all about breaking into them, like footwear. Getting pinched by a 3000 rupee bra (the most I have spent) is far worse than getting pinched by a 200 rupee bra you picked off the street just because it looked nice and was purple. You sort of feel obliged to give it another shot: maybe I am PMSing and therefore bloated, so it feels uncomfortable, maybe I need to break into it, maybe I am not breathing properly, may be something is wrong with my posture. But sometimes it's just not meant to be – you and the bra.

Apart from rib slicing and welt production, poking out is another chief problem with underwire bras. Again, no one was talking about it. The difference between 'any bra' and an underwire bra was that it had bones. And if you have ever dissected an underwire bra, like I have (several times), you will know what I mean.

Once after fidgeting an entire day, I went home, and in a fit of rage decided to rip open my underwire bra, just to attack the source of the constant attack. What I found was devastating. Burrowed deep inside (I had to use a paper cutter, since scissors couldn't dig deep enough, and this is because it was an expensive bra that I had sacrificed buying a pair of jeans for) was a treacherous steel rim. Sharp enough and resilient enough to kill a human being. I had been wearing this human bomb for months now! No wonder I felt what I felt. If this is the price to pay for womanhood, I quit.

So one day, I got myself a Sinead O'Connor haircut, threw my bra and showed up at work. Fuck the décolletage, I said. Hello gravity!

I was then an advertising copywriter at Ogilvy and Mather. One day, I found my boss looking not at me, but slightly lower when I was discussing an idea and I realised later that he knew my secret because the evening silhouette in his cabin had revealed my nipples (although I was careful to wear a shirt with pockets, to, you know, add a layer?) I am most certain he was gazing through my (busy) shirt at my nipples. Next thing I know, I am invited to an out of town pitch where he chose to drive and play all my favorite RD Burman songs on loop and when in Pune (where the pitch was) he asked if I wanted to come over to his room for a drink. I ran of course.

The next day, I went back to bra-torture.

My hostel life was about encountering several women with bra panache. They all waltzed in and out, their breasts singing (the underwire effect I assumed) and they all looked elegant and poised in whatever they wore, and I never saw anyone fidget. I continued to be miserable and waiting to get home so I could take my bra off. I noticed that the larger the women were, the less they fidgeted. You know, the ones who you would think will have to roll over their breasts separately when they roll over in bed? They seemed most comfortable. How, I wondered. Did they not find the weight and the bra tug unbearable?

The most unforgettable one among them was Shilpi, who had seven colors for seven days and she usually washed them all on Sunday (where the legend was that she went bra-less). I had heard it often enough to want to go and sneak up on her, which I did one day under the pretext of wanting to borrow acetone. And there I saw it! Flamboyant, padded, laced and redolent, her weapons of mass destruction stood (or hung) in all their glory on her towel rod. There was no element of self-consciousness, embarrassment or coyness about their full frontal display. This is where I want to get with my bras, I thought. Shilpi was my new hero. I wanted to give my bras full clothes line status and not dry them in a dingy corner of the bathroom where they were hidden from all.

The thing about wearing a really good-looking bra that makes you want to not wear clothes over it (it was that good-looking), is that it is often welt-inducing as well and at some point during the day, you want to take it off real bad. You usually have to wait till the end of the day, but keep fantasizing about how good it will feel when it actually comes off. I have often taken off excruciating bras while driving back home, and once, even in a cab, when I could bear it no more. The sign of true friendship is when you take off your bra from under your t-shirt when you are with her. Sometimes you do it even as you are ringing her bell. My roommate and I could compete for "who can take their bra off from under any item of clothing in less than 10 seconds".

The point of lingerie was that it had to look so delicious that a suitable man (or woman) wanted to see more of you. Only, that meant having to endure it till you managed to convince someone that you were so much fun on the outside that they couldn't wait to explore your insides. This is often a very slow process, and until then you had to "wear the right bra"! The underlying assumption always when you wore a fancy bra is that someone else would unhook it for you and that someone would be the object of your dreams. And that someone would have read the bra unhooking manual, because it's so uncool to unhook your own bra, at least when the sexcapade has just started.

As the years progressed and I continued to suffer, the buzzwords were sexy, demi cup, seamless, pushup, and whatnot. The LaSenza brigade had arrived and women were shopping for bras like they were buying candy. I joined the bandwagon too, and always came with a bag full of candy that was great to look at, and felt good at the trial, but every time I wore one after getting home, I felt the same.

It's not comfortable, you tell the bra-expert at the lingerie store and she will say, dismissively, "Have you tried adjusting the strap?" What she means is: have you tried to defy gravity even further? So you keep adjusting the next row of eyes and pull the straps tighter, so now the focus is not just on the underwire cutting through your ribs, but on you being suspended from up above, like meat hanging off a hook in a butcher's shop. But gravity always gets its way. Not that I had much to fear, because at 32B your stakes are still low. If the band felt okay, the cups were loose. If the cups felt ok, the band choked me. And yes, I had optimized all the hooks by then. And when I complained, women gave me the look of "Oh your poor thing!"

I figured I had to go through life suffering DEATH BY BRA, and perhaps I will find my calling someday. I am still waiting.

Along the way I did meet one or two contenders that I felt I could never let go of; they eventually met the fate that most bras meet – they got worn out and died and I could never replace them.

My 32Bs had a happy journey being unhooked regularly by suitable and unsuitable men till my 34 B life stage which is when I got married. With that, the whole torture-bra wearing pressure came down a little and I could afford to be lax, for lack of a better word.

And then just like that, I was pregnant and 34C. Now there was what you might call an exponential growth. Not to mention the fact that now I was asked to formally wean off the underwire bra (there was a deluge of cancerous reports). But I had moved on and embraced maternity bras.

Hello! What's THAT?

If you want to study bra technology in fine detail, you cannot miss maternity bras. Picture having garters for your breasts, except they are the most unaesthetic, scary looking things that help unclip your cups for easy nursing.

When I went to buy them, I dreamt purple and fuchsia pink and plum red (I must admit, my breasts looked really nice during my pregnancy, I was for once, feeling very feminine, and hence the aspiration for aforementioned colors).

In the most boring, industrial-looking corner of the store was the bra section. I was thrust two packets. Black and beige. What about colors, I asked? No colors, I was told with a stern face. I settled for one of each.

I must say that they were the most comfortable (and therefore most unsexy) bras I have ever worn; I continued wearing them much after I stopped nursing, because I was so scared to go bra shopping again and I was loathe to part with them.

I had reached the zenith of my braspiration if there can be such a thing.

If bras were not enough torture, there was the added pressure of having to wear strapless bras for all those off shoulder tops and tube dresses, at least the time when they were 'in'. Now of course it's totally okay to wear a strapless dress with a regular bra (or maybe it's still not ok, but I have stopped caring). I remember paying a huge sum of money once to buy a strapless bra (36 pounds, M&S, London) and still feeling insecure about keeping my assets in place as my strapless bra (yes, the same one I paid 36 quid for) often headed south after a rigorous session on the dance floor or sometimes, even a good joke. Once on a particularly boozy and dancy Friday, my strapless bra and the funky tunic over it rode southwards enough to unleash one of my brownies. I thought no one noticed, but then as I pulled my bra and top over my modesty, I made eye contact with the object of someone else's affection and he turned his interest to me the rest of the evening, and I went back to what I did best. Fidgeting.

I hear that to combat accidents such as the one above, Wonderbra recently unveiled its finger design underwear, designed to mimic the lift that women often resort to, to hold up their boobies. The bra has been designed to mimic the ideal lift and support achieved when women hold up their own bust with the help of a brand new structure shaped with four 'fingers' that is moulded into each cup. It seems underwire is so yesterday. Now I hear there are things like Bravity – a night bra that prevents formation of creases and wrinkles on your cleavage. When does it ever end?

Even after my lactating breasts settled back into 34B, I postponed getting back to a regular bra as long as I could, opting to wear dresses with empress cuts, moving to sarees (so my breasts could breathe free in the katori cut saree blouse), or just wearing layers. But eventually my bra crusade began again, and right now, I am holding on to a fuchsia bra and another denim Triumph both of which fit snug as a bug and feel like friends that I never want to lose. The other instruments of torture still sit and wait their turn in my drawer while I dabble with stick-ons and other non-invasive boob-traps and still get conned into a bra that announces itself as non-wired, full-cup, total support. I start feeling the spasm in my back the next day and shoot off a mail to Marks and Spencer, suggesting to them that they should get their designs clinically tested. They of course cheerily offer me a replacement.

I thought my struggles with the bra are over that I had finally made peace with it. But every time I venture on getting a new bra, it feels like a new relationship – it feels like too much work and getting used to, and I am better off without it. I am choosing comfort over adventure, and I hope it is just a phase.

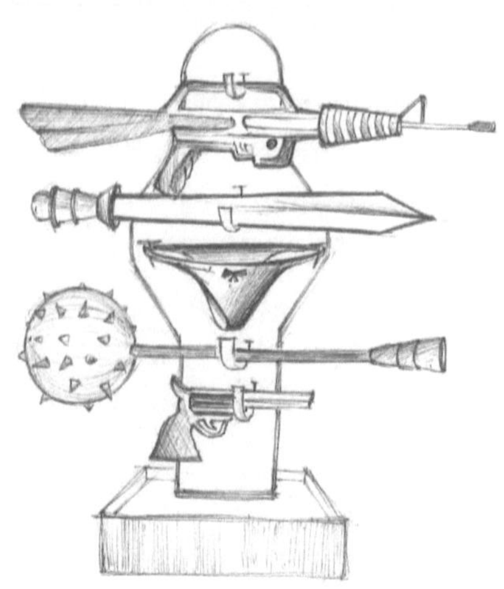

# 4. Thongs and other weapons of crotch destruction

Here's the thing. From the time I left school (when all my underwear decisions or the lack of them were my mother's), I have been looking for a decent pair of panties that are not welt-inducing, that have enough fabric to cover my vagina and both buttocks, that come in happy colors, stay in place and don't wander off, pinch, wedge or hurt me in any way.

I used to be XS and have grown up to be an M but my panty woes have more or less been the same. Except at the time, I would actually buy from the children's section and found that the panties for 12-14 year old girls were super comfortable and came in cheery colours too. And then one day I grew an ass and I was so frustrated trying to find a good, sensible, comfortable pair of panties that I stopped wearing one for a good six months. Just like I stopped wearing a bra.

I notice women of different sizes and shapes have different needs, but they are often unified by their frustration at not being able to find a decent pair of panties (or knickers if you prefer that term). It illustrates the true meaning of solidarity as does the inability to find a decent pair of period panties.

If research estimates the woman's underwear market in India at a whopping 11 crores (I am not usually good at dropping statistics like this, but this number stayed with me), why on earth is it so difficult for me to find a decent pair of panties? I can't believe that India's designers are making clothes for Michelle Obama and Judi Dench and yet no one has seen this huge gap in the market and has ventured into making well-designed, well-fitting, comfortable panties

I want a few pairs of soft, comfortable cotton panties (because I like some oxygen for my vagina) that I can grab and put on and waltz through my day. Preferably in fun colors. Not grey. Not maroon. Not shit green. I have tried everything from the Rs 50 a piece to Rs 799 (the most I ever paid for something to cover my crotch), I have tried low waist, high waist, bikini, comfort, seamless, shorts, and always felt that perhaps it was my body and its sudden ampleness that made it complicated.

And then I wondered. Is it only my ample rear that is struggling with finding a good pair of panties? Am I the only one trying to unwedge my wedgies all the time? Are the stick insects waltzing through life, their derriere hugged by the most comfortable panties that they slip in and out of? Or are they all wearing thongs?

I can't say I was relieved to find that everyone had the same issues. Except that, like the bra solidarity brigade, no one was talking about it. Imagine if men had underwear issues! There would be war.

Your panties have a lot of work to do. They have to help you negotiate the world and all its eccentricities and irregularities and hang in there (hopefully without added colours and fluids) until you get back home and throw them in the wash (they need their down time too, and I cannot stress enough on the importance of sleeping without underwear).

During my pregnancy I switched to wearing men's underwear and realised how comfortable they were. I was also envious how men simplistically fit into two boxes – boxers and briefs. But then I was told men have their own issues about underwear, but let someone else write about that.

And why is it so tough to get panties right? There are just a few basic requirements, right?

1. Like they should have enough fabric to cover both your buttocks. It's amazing how hard it is to get this right. Most underwear in the market is shrinking in size so fast, you will need a magnifying lens to even look at them in some time.
2. They shouldn't give you a wedgie. Because much productive time is lost either training the mind to get used to the feeling or finding a spot to unwedge your butt.
3. They shouldn't pinch your skin. You don't want to be sitting through a meeting and then be seized by a desire to unpanty yourself because you have been seriously injured by elastic on your hips.
4. Panties should not have a mind of their own. By this I mean they shouldn't be wandering off or rolling down and settling anywhere they feel like.
5. The last thing a panty should be is a pain in the ass.

At some point, I think a shoe manufacturer lost his way into making panties. Because they suddenly started coming with tie ups, added flaps, ruffles in the front, random lace sticking out on the sides, bows in the rear and all sorts of anomalies. It's a panty for fuck's sake, not a ballerina pump for a four year-old girl.

### Honey, I shrunk my panty!

Initially, when you are still this gawky person who has just started to have an income and are struggling with non-issues like visible panty line, you will find a friend who says, "Have you tried thongs? They are the best. You feel like you are wearing nothing."

Everyone falls for this and it's absolutely untrue and everyone wonders if they are the only ones who feel like they have got a permanent wedgie or their butts are being flossed constantly. But no woman dares to say that thongs make her truly squirm.

Thongs used to be things you are supposed to wear when you are hoping (or planning) to get some action. Except I would usually take them off before I got the action, that is how torturous they were. If thongs were unbearable, there came crotchless panties. If this is what it took to get action, I don't want any of it. And besides, men don't really give a shit about what kind of panties you are wearing. They are just grateful you want to take them off for them.

When I confessed my thong issues to a friend, she told me in the manner of thong-divas to thong-nots: may be you are wearing the wrong kind? Have you tried La Senza? So then I quickly rushed to the La Senza store and spent a small fortune on buying the 'right thongs'. Except they felt the same. And I felt poorer. Also I know by now that VPL is overrated. I am sure the term was invented by the makers of thongs.

I believe thongs must be weapons of torture in some parts of the world. If ordinary panties give you a wedge, thongs take it to another level. Because here, there is certainly something that is planted between your buttocks which is threatening to migrate into your innards, given enough time. Trying thongs is not like trying tampons. Unlike tampons, that don't remind you of your menstrual flow every time you visit the loo, thongs are unable to make you feel that you are not wearing panties (in fact it is the exact opposite).

The other problem (however basic) I have with thongs is not being able to tell the front side from the rear. Why should this be so hard without the label?

According to research, wearing a thong isn't excellent for your vagina if you're prone to vaginal infections. They apparently open the windows to all kinds of bacteria. I know this is too much information, but I am trying to do a good deed here. I would any day choose visible panty line over a crotch infection. Or stick to thongs only for the high-fashion days.

Also, wearing thongs is not as easy breezy as those stick insects on the ramp or lingerie models make it seem. There's this constant strange sensation of fresh (or not so fresh) air on your bottom when they're worn with skirts or dresses. You feel naked and not in a good way.

Last I heard, more and more men are opting to have sex with women who believe in comfort over style. The thong – once the epitome of sexy lingerie – is on the decline among young women; more and more of them choose full-coverage, often high-waisted underwear. May be granny panties will bring another kind of sexy back.

Bloody hell! After I wasted my youth on the blasted things.

I am so done with thongs. At the tender age of 48, I no longer have to subject my vagina and my butt to a permanent floss. The few thongs I still possess lie buried in my underwear drawer as 'in case of emergency' panties. Like the time I don't do laundry for days and have to travel suddenly.

As I get older, I am always craving clothes and shoes that allow me to live my life free, unfettered, unburdened by the constant need to check and tweak and check again. Someone please make some good, comfortable panties soon! I want to try at least a dozen colours before I die. I don't want to feel that between wearing the wrong panties and the wrong bras, my life is over.

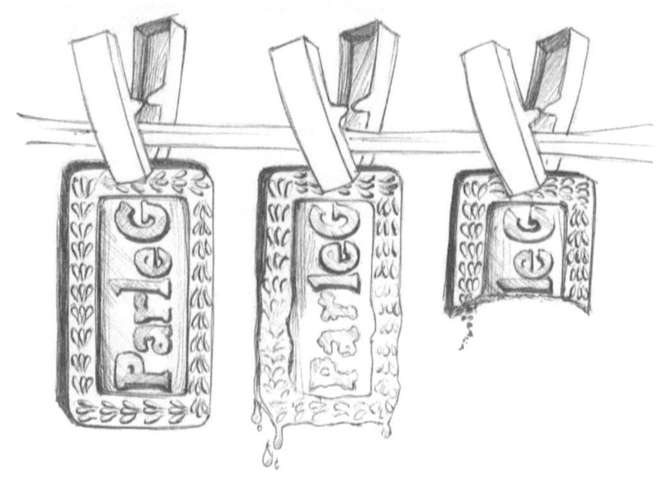


# 5. Food as memory: The art of cooking and feeding

I can always count on food.

It triggers memory. It helps fill in the details. It assures me that it happened.

For almost every important memory I have, there is a smell to go with it, and a taste. I don't know if that's the case for everyone, but there are certain things from a long time ago that I can taste right now, although there is no way I can ensure they taste the same. Most of them don't exist.

Like I'm sure Incremin doesn't. When I was three or four was when Incremin came home. It was one of those height-inducing tonics, or so it said on the cover. An amber coloured flattish bottle with a rectangular base and a tall neck. If that was not enough of a visual mnemonic for height, there was a picture of an unusually happy giraffe on it. It was my father's idea. Appa always wanted me to grow up tall, like him. He is six feet tall, even with his stoop at 78 now, and I was a puny child from the start (and haven't grown much vertically since). Incremin was delicious and I didn't much care for height, but I gulped it everyday.

I was the first-born, so I guess I got the best deal on all the goodies and tonics. The twins came four years later and by then, there was no Incremin budget. In any case, my brother got the height from the genes eventually and so it all went well.

Childhood was also about Parle G, and no, it's not the same, although it's still around (albeit in 100% plastic that makes no attempt to even match the wax-coatedness of the wrapper then). When you opened a packet of Parle G those days, you didn't know what you were getting. Sometimes, you got the just-burnt-enough-to-be-extra-scrumptious biscuits. Sometimes you got the ones that tasted just like you remembered them and were exciting in a let-me-quickly-dunk it in my tea way. After years of eating Parle G biscuits, I once got the chance to live next door to where they were made. My best friend in college, Vidu, lived at the Principal's quarters close to the Parle G factory and we often studied together. The whiff of Parle G, although an exciting thing to wake up to, had me feeling nauseous by the third time I went over for a weekend of study. I could never eat the biscuits with the same degree of nostalgia after that.

Another thing Appa indulged us with when we were little was Ovaltine. It was the Bournvita of my childhood. It had a powdery, muddy texture to it and the chocolate was more in your face than camouflaged malt drinks of today. It sort of spoke to you and said that you are never too young to appreciate good chocolate.

Many Ovaltines later when we children still didn't look well-fed enough, Appa gave up and left it to nature. Ovaltine was gone by then, and somehow the sterile Complan, which was Amma's choice, never appeared nostalgia-worthy.

While the Ovaltine and Incremin were staples, Appa's food purchases were quite predictable depending on the time of the month. Week one of his salary was completely binge time. There were cheeselings, marshmallows, nankhatais from Cheddas's, soup cubes (which we at the time didn't know were chicken and always licked the bowl clean when Appa made soup with it). Soup day was always a special day and we never imagined it would feel so posh, just the four of us sitting down and having soup from bowls and with soup spoons (I think Amma smelt the chicken part and decided to turn all Brahmin on us and stayed away). When Appa was in an extra generous mood, he would toss in the croutons (fried in ghee, no less) and the aroma was like sleeping in a really lovely crib with those things hanging that we only saw in pictures. Some days, there was cassata ice-cream or kulfi (always in three flavours), plus chocolate bars (transparent inside and solid chocolate outside), and always flowers for Amma (mogra, yards of it).

But the world became a more beautiful place the day Appa learnt to make pavbhaji. It was the eighties and pavbhaji was just in. I was ten at the time and the twins were six. Appa came home one day with some capsicum, peas, cauliflower, a whole block of butter (butter was a big deal for us, we were never a bread family) and a magical pouch that said 'Everest PavBhaji masala'. He never pressure-cooked the vegetables (he doesn't, even now). He would gently boil them in the order of their mashworthiness (so the potatoes went in first, then the cauliflower and the peas and lastly the capsicum). Then he would take a huge slab of butter and toss it on the tava and gently sautee the onions and then in went the tomatoes and lots of pavbhaji masala and finally the other vegetables, awaiting their turn patiently. Appa also made his buttered masala pavs with secret ingredients that we still don't know, but all I know is we ate and ate and never wanted to wash out mouth after. Those were the days Appa cooked all the gourmet stuff and Amma, the regular stuff.

We had pavbhaji on the first two Saturdays of the month and by the third, Appa never had money for butter and Amma didn't want to spend her money on something as wasteful as butter. Pavbhaji has become passè since then and I may have had thousands of them, but in Appa's version, each vegetable got its share of the limelight. He was always fair to his produce, I will give that to him.

In the summer holidays, we went cousin-trotting all over Bombay, spending a week or two at the house my maternal grandmother currently lived in (usually one of my uncles). Often at mealtimes (usually dinner), she would ask us to form a circle and announce that it was *tuthu* night. We didn't realise then that this was a ploy to make a frugal meal sound exciting. Tuthu is when you were hand-fed from a large utensil filled with rasam rice or sambar rice. It had huge logistical advantages of minimising utensils, laying the table, cleaning up after and other such, and killed several birds (or mouths) with one stone. Usually my grandmother had her favourite stories saved for tuthu time. I still remember one whodunit type of story featuring a quarter crook, half crook, three quarter crook and full crook. We had to guess who was the ace crook and why. Till the end, she never told us who she thought was the best strategist and each time we guessed, she would ask us to rethink. Her story telling sessions often made us forget that we didn't want to eat the 'boring food' in the first place. Those of us who ate quickly got a reward of an extra crispy (vadam) when no one was looking.

It's exciting, although tricky to grow up in a household where both your parents are excellent cooks. We inadvertently ended up passing verdicts on whose preparation was better. Appa always excelled in the pachadis, avials, kootus and curries, while there was no competition for Amma in her sambars, idlis, chutneys, thokkus and pickles. Plus Appa had the added advantage of buying things off the rack which the purist in Amma would never allow. Even tomato ketchup had to be made at home and we have spent many winters sterilising bottles and ladling up Amma's home-made ketchup into them. At Rs 10 a kilo (or whatever ridiculous price she got the tomatoes for), she calculated that we had saved hundreds of rupees on ketchup. Of course, every other snack she made was always served with ketchup, because she had to justify 12-14 bottles of it at home. Also, a non-bread family such as ours suddenly started buying loaves of bread to make sandwiches and other such alien things. Soon, the ketchup bottles were doled out to any willing visitor and we heaved a sigh of relief.

The difference between Appa and Amma cooking is, Amma's food always tastes the same in a delicious, comforting, reassurance of home way. With Appa, you have to take your chances. He will never make the same thing in the same way (at least he hasn't in the last 10 years during which he has been cooking almost exclusively at home). Even when we travelled, Amma could never fathom why we always went to remote, unheard of places like Dhanolti and Kasauni while everybody else went to Nainital and Shimla. "Why can't we just go to a place people have heard of?" she would say.

When we would return from these trips, completely broke, (thanks to Appa's 'live for the moment' ideology), sometimes we would just have enough to get into an auto or tempo and reach home. Amma would always make a *vettalkozhambu* in the middle of the night with hot steamed rice. Sometimes, if we were lucky, there were onions that survived the trip and went into the *kozhambu*. We ate like we were just reborn. Amma saved us, although Appa took us on the real adventures. Amma always showed us that there was a place for wisdom and prudence in this world.

I don't think any man I dated or was in a relationship with supplied me as many food memories as my father. May be that's why I never had trouble moving on, because as long as there were no major food memories, it was easy to get up and go. Except perhaps with Roger, Beeps and Matt.

Roger, who was Swedish, made me the gentlest European vegetarian fare over wood fires during our romance in the wilderness of Kerala. The omelettes he made (because he was concerned I wasn't getting enough protein), were spiced so delicately, I forgot I was eating eggs. We cooked a lot together, and made mixtapes and I still believe that it is never possible to have nothing to talk about when you have food in common. Food horoscopes are my plan for compatibility.

Beeps was a Sikh surgeon who rode a bike and could cook. Whenever Beeps sauteed asparagus with butter and had a bottle of red wine and a candle ready, I knew the night had potential. But Beeps was as good for an afternoon jhalmuri and beer as he was for dinners.

Matt had me at vadapav. He was as American as it gets and on our first date, he was making vadapavs for a party of expats and they were all gushing about him. I had the audacity to point out the difference between using whole coriander seeds and dhania-jeera powder off the shelf. He was hooked. And then he never stopped cooking for me. Tsatsiki with dill, rasbhari salads with feta and arugula, his special sauteed spinach with lemon and garlic, tabouleh with dalia, watermelon and tomato salad with red wine vinegar or pumpkin quiche and of course sangria. I now know it was never the food. It was what Matt did to them.

When I broke up with him, I knew I wouldn't meet someone who had such a repertoire and love for cooking. I didn't.

Dee, the man I married, loved my salads, pastas, bakes and dips. On our first date, I served him roasted baby potatoes in thyme, spinach soup, garlic bread and cheese and olive sticks with Glenmorangie. He polished it all off and the date lasted nine hours with no hankypanky. That was big for both of us and told us may be this was the real deal. A year into our marriage, Dee told me that he is a strict non-vegetarian and doesn't like vegetables. I must say I was a tad taken aback. I did try making him chicken in garlic sauce, 'just like his mother's', and once for his birthday – my friend Maria's chicken in yogurt gravy. The whole world sighed and told him it was true love. I don't know much about love, but yes, I am good with food. And adapting to a loved one. Frying sausages became as common as frying onions for the vegetarian me.

I find it easier to be friends with people who love to eat or cook. Even today, my friends are what they cook or feed. Rashna, my agony aunt always had a door open and a shoulder to cry on during my messy youth. She was a Parsi who had married into a Gujarati household and their kitchen table reminded me of my grandmother and her large heart. The household help Narangseth would make the most lovely crispy aloos and bhindis and really simple gujrati dals and phulkas with ghee. When they bought their own place and moved away from the family home, a part of me knew that their table would never be so full again. First of all, there wasn't space to put a real table in a one BHK. Second, it was a luxury to have full-time help in a tiny flat. I was right.

I know my friends by their equation with food. Farzana never liked to cook, but she always made this lovely teheri (a rice dish with aloo) which was so flavourful and pure, just like her soul. There is Rama who prided herself at never stepping into the kitchen but knew exactly the way to my heart. Her table was laden and the conversations were always luscious and continue to be, twenty years later. Sapan was as elaborate and methodical in her cooking as she was scattered and confused in her life. In her food, there was order, poise, elegance, whether a wild rice salad, herbed rice, pasta salad, or her avocado-crusted bread. Samina was as elegant in her kitchen as she was in real life and her mushroom-stuffed potatoes and stir fry with tofu peppers and greens in a lemon coriander sauce made me forget she is a strict carnivore. Sai turned bread into an art form, and there were no limits to her palate – peppers, caramelised onions, nigella seeds, sesame, cinnamon – the world was a happier place when she was proving her dough. Maria made me realise how much art there was in the simple boiling of a beetroot for her beetroot and watercress salad with the juice of a whole orange. Ophelia could transform the mundane slicing and sauteeing of onions and the crushing of ginger garlic into an act of supreme seduction just with her poise and charm.

People also became different people when they cooked. The hard-nosed Geeta who was always the career goddess once invited me over for counselling and fed me crispy hot karelas with lots of onions, rice and the most soulful yellow dal ever. I cannot erase the memory of that day, although I remember very little of our interactions otherwise. Or the practical and no-nonsense Dipti who induced pregnancy cravings in me by merely hinting at attasheera and dal dhokli which she whipped up in twenty minutes, as I sat in her sea-facing apartment, feeling my baby move with each lash of the waves.

I remember cooking with my friend Marguerite at Auroville's Mango guest house in Pondicherry, making a hearty pasta with salad, buying produce, pouring ourselves some wine, collectively lusting after a Frenchman who seemed to be cooking a rather elegant and elaborate meal all for himself in the community kitchen. I think it was a ratatouille, or something with a lot of eggplant in it. The 30s had set in and my hormones were wild for older men.

Marguerite and her husband Taba, were a truly bohemian, fun-loving couple with an absolutely wonderful home, in which everything had a story. Every ladle, every salad bowl, every placemat, cushion, sugar pot, tea infuser, rug, candle or diffuser. It's like their home was built over several hundred days, with much thought and love that went into each corner or wall and everything in between.

Their food was the same. There was never a pattern. Sometimes there was a hearty salad and soup with some freshly bought buns. Some days, when Taba was in the mood, there was Tadig, a fragrant Persian rice with a scrumptious golden brown crust. They was always a little something one of them had brought back from their many travels – a pickle, some apricot tea, some condiments, cheese, chocolate.

I find that food memories often have more texture and meaning than almost anything else. Very often I remember nothing of the places I visited, but I can taste them in my mouth. Like when we were kids and stranded at Dhanolti on a night without power (one of Appa's expeditions) and the kind caretaker of the lodge offered us a room and pakodas with chai for food. The crunchy capsicum and the cauliflower in the pakodas has been etched in my memory for life. I also remember the waiters at Nanu's in Naples who always allowed me to order just the sides (sauteed spinach, mushrooms, baby potatoes) when I felt I could actually make a meal of them. I remember eating injeras, robust and honest as they were, in 2000 on a Broadway walk (from South Ferry to the Bronx, no less) with Naresh and Anita in my wild single days. When I ate them again in 2014 with Abira, Antara and my almost five-year-old Rehaan, much had changed. I had turned from vagabond to woman to wife to mother. The injeras had also learnt how to repackage themselves and look cool. I missed them rustic though, like I missed me.

# 6. Woman and the art of maintenance

Sometimes I wish I could wake up as a woman instead of spending long hours transforming myself into one each day. I don't know how it is for the rest of you, but being able to balance my threading, waxing, pedicure and ovulation cycles in the most optimum way has always been one of the biggest challenges of womanhood for me. At times I feel that by the time you finally sync your waxing, threading, pedicure, manicure, facial, head massage and hair color (thankfully I opted out of that one)cycle, it's time for menopause.

I think of all those cumulative woman-hours spent getting my moustache done, getting my arms, legs and underarms waxed, threading my eyebrows and chin, tucking my pelvic wattle and other loosely hanging body parts into ridiculously expensive underwear before I was ready to step out into the world – and I think: what a colossal waste of time and money. There's too much admin in being a woman. Every heard of a man "getting stuff done" so he can be more man?

Let's face it. There are things you have to get done, simply to look like a woman or feel like one – some on a daily/weekly/monthly basis and I am talking basic epilatory stuff, not botox, liposuction and tummy tucks here. The irony is that by the time your body, skin, feet, nails and hair is in an optimum maintenance phase, there is a tiny window for you to display them and then you go back to where you started. Rinse, repeat.

As one grows older, it becomes an even bigger challenge balancing the outsides and insides (cysts, polyps, lumps, fibroids and their best friends suddenly come visiting). I have been told I must get a yearly pap smear and mammogram done and I have been putting it off because it's hard enough with the items already on the list.

Hair usually tops everyone's list and most of us have hair in more places than our mane to contend with and hence this section needed to be split:

## HAIR (everywhere)

Life is what happens between your waxing appointments. In the first week after your full body wax, which leaves you feeling soft and silky and woman all over, you usually find ways to bare as much skin as is possible (or your work place allows). In two weeks, the skirts get longer, or get replaced by trousers or jeans, the blouses get more conservative, and by the end of the six week period (usually prescribed for your next wax), you could well be wearing a tent.

The biggest preoccupation of my youth was: what if I meet someone really cute when I had just grown out my body hair for 'full-growth' and my appointment was still a week away? (The waxing lady at the parlour recommended this; once you had attained 'full growth', the hair came off really well on the wax strips, leaving no in-growths. Everyone knows the disgusted looks they are met with when you show up for a wax appointment with 'partial growth'.)

Needless to add, in the 'full growth and not yet waxed' phase, one is constantly on tenterhooks. What if things got hot and heavy with cute guy you just met and you ended up taking your clothes off in a room with bright lights? Just the thought of that happening was so scary that I made sure I never went anywhere close to any exciting places for fear of being caught in my hirsute condition. All possibility of action was stalled to keep up with my waxing appointment. For the most part, when one's hair, skin, feet are all perfect for display and the fuzz is under control on the eyebrows, upper lip, underarms, chin and pubis – it's a time bomb ticking away.

Will I have sex/meet someone nice to have sex with before this fabulous period expires?

Will I land an interview to my dream job?

Will I run into an ex who must see what a fabulous thing he let get away?

If these anxieties were not bad enough, along comes Carrie Bradshaw, announcing the Brazilian wax and how she felt like 'walking sex' after it. There was now one more item on the list and more and more women felt the push to rid themselves of their bush. I succumbed too, and spreading my legs to my waxing lady was something nothing had prepared me for. At the end of it, I don't remember if I felt like 'walking sex'; I did feel very tender and naked though and I remember my partner loved it. But before I went on to making this a part of the deal, I wanted to make sure it would be reciprocated. I waited a few months, and his bush didn't seem to go anywhere, so I went back to growing mine, pretending it was just a one-time treat.

And then there are moustaches to deal with.

I took my son with me to the beauty parlour once, when he was four. I had nowhere to leave him, and I had to get my moustache done. Yes, I have a moustache; my guess is I could have a beard too if I wait long enough.

*Where are we going mamma?*
*To the parlour.*
*Why?*
*I have to get my upper lip done.*
*What? But you already have an upper lip!*
*I have to get it threaded, so I don't grow a moustache.*
*But I thought girls don't have moustaches.*
*Well. There's a bit of boy in every girl. It's called testosterone.*
*Mamma, sometimes you say weird things.*

My homeopath once told me I had too much testosterone for a woman. She meant it in a diagnostic way; the way my yin and yang was a little off for a woman most of the time, and that loss in balance manifested itself in different ways. Moustache, for one.

No matter what I do, it sprouts out in a few days, so just when I am beginning to enjoy my moustache-free days, it's back again. For instance, if I am travelling abroad and don't want to waste precious dollars on hair removal, I get it threaded the day before I travel. But it's back like an old faithful by the time I cross the Pacific. I must confess I haven't tried laser as I somehow can't deal with the square-inch-by-square-inch epilation of my body and by the time the entire laserable surface area of my body is covered, I would have aged (which I anyway have, but that's beside the point). Also I have a friend whose upper lip laser went wrong and now she has a permanent mustache shadow on her upper lip. So it's threading, waxing and a combination thereof for me.

Perhaps a time will come when I will actually feel effortlessly woman. I am 48 now, and my sense is that it's nowhere close.

## NAILS

I have never been a mani-pedi girl. But the first time I got a pedicure, I realised how soft and gorgeous my feet felt and how, it was the one thing I could get done while still reading a book unlike other beauty parlour procedures that put you in dark rooms with a towel over your head and you not knowing where the switch to anything is. Pedicures are infinitely more fun than waxing where three women contort your body into different forms, make you stand with your head dangerously close to the ceiling fan and sometimes even flip around, as they simultaneously wax your arms and legs. Plus what I like about pedicures is being given such a wide choice of nail colour – it feels like a child being offered candy. So every time I went for a wax (which I had to), I threw myself a pedicure treat (which I wanted). As I left the parlour with bright shiny toe nails and kiss-worthy heels, all I could think of was how many open-toed shoes and sandals did I have to show them off. And how would I look wearing these open-toed sandals with some super short dresses, given that my freshly waxed legs were ready for display too. Even now, the pedicure happens only because I can get it to sync with my waxing cycle and it does feel good for a few days.

But, and this is something I never cracked: I was always wearing the wrong footwear the day I went for a pedicure which was a potential hazard to my freshly painted (and wet) nails. No matter how long I waited, or how careful I was, one or more toes were always stubbed by the time my feet got through and then had to be touched up. And once you know it has been touched up, and you are super careful about not destroying it any further it gets steadily worse.

But you keep treading daintily a day or two after your pedicure, and feeling all graceful and ladylike. Somehow manicures never had the same effect, or maybe I am more of a leg person. I did grow my finger nails and paint and file them when I was younger but I realised I was too clumsy to make a nail job last more than a few hours, so I gave up. A friend did tell me I should be a hand model, as I had fragile, delicate hands. I promptly ignored her. I never got into the manicure trap – I thought it was a thing for ladies who lunch. I liked my nails clean, and I occasionally filed, soaked and scrubbed them before painting them (I figured why pay someone when there were no cuticles to clean?). I did go through that phase of filing them square, when square was in, until I began to lose track of what was in. Plus I like to cook, which ladies who get manicures usually don't.

I now see there are more nail bars than beauty parlours and it must mean something, but I have a child now, and am worried about hurting him, so it's back to school girl nails and one less item on the maintenance list.

## BODY

I often look back in nostalgia at the body of my twenties and thirties. I didn't think much of it then, but I long for it now. It was the time I was lithe, had great limbs, a real waist and a chiseled face and was mostly fit and could have worn practically anything. Except I thought I needed to fill out more, get more curves, be more woman.

Now I am too much woman although the limbs are still good, but the middle is a contentious zone. I have also learned to look at my body as a whole and not the sum of its parts. I am celebrating drop waist dresses, unstructured fits and of course, the world's best camouflage – sarees. I hate cinching and I am too lazy to try to appear thinner than I am.

Arundhati Roy was on the cover of Elle recently, and what struck me the most about her interview was the revelation that she was 54 and she goes to the gym every single day. Every. Single. Day. Frankly, it made me more envious of her than her Booker prize or how she wore marriage so lightly and divorce even lighter. I thought of other women who were struggling to stay attractive at 54, 44, 34 and even 24. Women who were dealing with issues of body image, ageing, hormones and other womanly problems; what set Roy apart was that she had decided to show up.

Showing up is harder than we think. I have realised that any form of exercise linked to short term goals (have to lose x kg, have to fit into that dress, have to look good in gymwear, have to look fit at my wedding) never works. Exercise is a tribute you pay to your body every day. Every single day.

The point is: we may or may not be happy with our bodies, but we all need exercise. Some of us, like my father, get it without being aware of it. My dad is a farmer; he works the land, he walks everywhere he can walk to, carries his own luggage and still fits into clothes from twenty years ago. Others, like me, struggle to keep our date with exercise. I actually love the idea of it, I think about it much more than I do it. I am a good starter of things, but lack consistency of purpose. Maybe I live in hope that my genes will take care of the discrepancies.

But consistency is the real talent. It's where we have to get at. Doing the same thing every day, or a few times a week, takes a special kind of discipline. Whenever I find myself at a park in the morning and see more old people than young – walking, running, doing yoga, laughter therapy or whatever, I feel inspired. These people are good at showing up. And showing up is very overrated in today's world, because the easier thing to do is not leave your house (or smart phone) at all.

I don't remember doing much to stay fit in my twenties; it was my thirties where I really pushed my body into various physically grueling forms – I took up Iyengar Yoga, joined a gym, learned to swim and cycle, took jazz ballet and hiphop lessons. I was determined to be a fit 40, and I was. And then I let it all slide. Wait a minute. It was my uterus.

Until I gave birth, my daddy's genes were all with me. But once my body was turned inside out by pregnancy and motherhood, things looked far tougher and I realised exercise was something I really needed to factor in. With pregnancy and turning 40 and all the body and hormonal and life changes that came with it, I lost my mojo. I let my body go, I kept lowering the bar and then one day, I found myself in Landour, walking with my six year-old and realised I couldn't keep up. We were walking a lot on that holiday and my son was beating me hollow.

I have been walking a lot lately. It's something I have arrived at by elimination: Swimming is a production; you need to wear a costume and show up at the pool at a designated time, you can't really swim at will. Running is something that makes me overwhelmed; I clearly don't have the stamina for it yet, but I will get to it sometime. Yoga needs a class and I'm fussy about my brand of yoga. I always thought I am not a 'walk person', more a run or dance or cycle person. But my body says otherwise and I have finally decided to listen to it.

I look at walking as something that can be done anywhere, with minimal planning. You can walk even if you don't have the right kind of walking shoes, or don't have a park next to you. You simply have to decide that you are going to get from point A to point B. And you have to start somewhere.

If walking around aimlessly or wandering would qualify as an exercise, I think I may have done a few marathon equivalents of those. To make it interesting (and since I'm not the kind of person who can walk round and round a park every day), I take a different route each day. Walking has introduced me to parts of my neighbourhood I would have never discovered driving around in my car or jumping into an auto. It has been alone time of a different kind.

The gym I found to be the most distracting and least productive compared to all exercise forms I have tried so far. It was always about how you looked, what you wore, what did your body smell of, why does everyone else's exercise gear always look more exciting, how do some women manage to look so hot working out and I don't, why do I perspire so much? And why do people take so many selfies in the gym? Clearly my gym is not as inspiring as Roy's, although it has all the equipment.

I read an interesting post about exercising on Huffington post which said that the person who wears shoes is as much a contender for exercise as someone who has been hitting the gym for years. I guess I finally make the cut.

### HAIR (head)

It is strange that I found myself roughly the same time as I found my hair.

I have a point here. If there can be a human mascot for tropical, evergreen, deciduous forests, it is my family. Each one of us has been blessed with manes that will pass down to at least three generations irrespective of who we marry.

I remember feeling like a gawky adolescent, in my thin frame and ample, curly, unruly, jet black mane, rendered into two braids. I would sigh at the girls in my class who tossed their hair from side to side with the mere flick of a chin, and whose ponytails bounced as they ran. Leaving my hair loose was considered an invitation to the demons, so even on the hair-wash days, it was tied when semi-dry so it wouldn't blow up into an unnecessary balloon. I silently wished that I would undergo a genetic transformation and wake up one morning with silken tresses that would toss all over your face when you did suitable dance moves or made love.

But as a young person, I was quite inarticulate about my hair potential and got reasonably tongue-tied when it came to discussing the cut with the stylist. "Whatever you think will look good," is normally what we are programmed to tell our hairdressers, thanks to our mothers. Mine would add, "Do something that will make her look soft and gentle."

As I grew older, and the hair wilder (they no longer had to be plaited), there were jibes at every corner: Do you use conditioner?

When was the last time you oiled your hair?

Have you combed it?

It's so rough, no?

You have so much hair! How do you manage? Why don't you try straightening?

After being apologetic for years, I finally mustered the courage one day to say, "No, because I enjoy being me. Because people are paying serious money all over the world to be me. Because I don't know anyone like me."

It was the time when curls were hot. So was dusky. I had both. I was finally hot!

The whole hairstylist thing is a bit like the dating game. You go out with different people – some you never want to meet again, some you give a second chance to, some you might move from coffee to lunch to dinner with, some who will never cease to remind you how the others messed you up. Some who make you feel that they are the only ones you can trust. And some, you can perhaps live happily ever after with. As long as I lived with my parents, every haircut (rather, hair experiment) was met by a cold stare from my parents and a look of awe from a few cousins (I suspect because I dared to do what they couldn't).

After much trial and some glaring errors, I found Raul Miranda who turned out to be the man who re-baptized me.

The first thing he said was, "Wow, this is wild—I love your hair. There's so much you can do with it." The lock-chop resulting in a fido-dido look did great things for me, but most importantly, I felt redeemed, liberated, alive. My curls sprang back as though released from years of bondage. It was truly an unbearable lightness of being. He also taught me that curly hair's best friend is fingers. And worst enemy - the comb. He introduced me to product. I soon learnt the fine art of scrunching.

Every six weeks, I was back at his door. In the meantime, he had acquired an American wife and a brood of bulldogs. In a year he was off to the prosperous climes of New York and never came back. And I was left wild-haired and nowhere to go. The next few years were a series of unfortunate events packed with as many wrong guys as wrong hairdressers. My hair went through a long and arduous journey, trying to resist the lures of straightening, extensore, rebonding and what not. Luckily, I learnt from others' mistakes.

It was also the time my mum was lining up suitable boys for me, and was obviously cross that I had destroyed my biggest asset, that too, when I was threateningly close to 30. But I was beyond caring. Finally, I had found the freedom to be me, and was at a point where I could celebrate my hair, and more importantly, me.

After Raul left, I had no one who got my hair, so I let it grow all the way down to my waist and finally met Avani – a hair dresser of my dreams who totally got curls. I was happy in the head again (which is also the name of her salon, by the way).

I totally get it when your biggest concern while moving cities or countries is whether or not you will find a hairdresser that gets your hair. It's a big deal – hair, especially if you have too much of it (like I do) or too little. The ones in between can safely cushion a botch up, but not the ones who need dilution or concentration.

But then we all have had our share of hairum-scarrum stories, and people have trampled all over our hair insecurities. Most times, we are lured into spending huge amounts of money on our hair only to end in total wreckage.

My son has inherited my hair, and his luscious curls always stand out in a monochrome of straight or blandly wavy-haired kids. But luckily, I am not my mother, so he will receive the gentle loving care of fingers and will be well protected from the evil effects of the comb and brushes and other objects that purport to tame, but end up with disastrous effects.

In my forties, I finally let go of my curls. They had given me much. Now it was time to say goodbye and adopt my pixie, as it was more becoming of my salt-n-pepper. Someone told me I was the straight version of Ellen Degeneres and I thought that was cool. Other friends said I was a female George Clooney. I think I'll keep both.

I finally wake up feeling like a million bucks. There are no more bad hair days. I am a get up and go girl. For the most part. I miss the curls though.

## HAIR COLOUR

I get that look a lot nowadays, especially when I am with child in tow. Perhaps it has to do with my pixie crop and the fact that my greys are in their full nakedness – all there for everyone to comprehend, theorize, extrapolate – and the look in their eyes seems to say, "How did she manage to wing that?"

I am convinced this whole greying business is a big deal.

Here is the thing: If you are over 35 and have no greys showing, you are definitely colouring (barring very few exceptions).

My mother started colouring her hair (henna mostly) in solidarity when various aunts (even uncles) took to it with much vigour as their daughters and sons were getting married and they wanted to 'look young' in photos. They still colour: it looks pathetic, with their sagging skin, warts and tired eyes, but now it would be too sudden to reverse the process, so as they say, they are 'stuck'. Thankfully my mother stopped colouring when she realised I wasn't going to.

Many of my friends are 'stuck' because it seems (and one of them told me this) if they stop, their children will think they have aged suddenly and are going to die. They colour so their children think they are young and cool and most importantly not going to die anytime soon.

There are always reasons to opt for hair colour, and they will always seem valid. In the beginning, you color because well, why should everyone know you are greying (read ageing)? Then you colour because your family has got used to your dark mane, and now you don't want to shock. Then you colour because you have a child and you want her to think her mother is still young, like 'all other mothers'. Then you colour because you don't want to look older than your husband or your sister-in-law. Or you colour because you want your team at work to think that you are one of them. Or you colour because your publisher thinks it is good for the image of the magazine you edit.

My friends succumbed – either to emotional blackmail or a job which prescribed they look a certain way. Then there are the halfway house kinds – the ones who'll streak, not do a 'global' colouring, or the ones that will wear their hair in a way that the least greys show. The real problem with colouring is that you can never stop. Your hair is always eager to show its true self, and so the roots peep out in two weeks, announcing: This is the real me! And then quickly, the curator in you shuts it down by 'touching it up', asking it to blend in and be like the one you want to be.

Rinse, repeat.

They say 40 is the new 30. Or 50 is the new 40. But women still want to look 35 at 40. Or 60 at 70. They can, with hair colour. Who am I to stop that? I just wanted to reduce one aspect of maintenance, and my grey pixie suits me just fine.

## SKIN

The day I came to terms with the fact that I would never have a flawless complexion was the most liberating day of my life. I have bad skin. If you were to analyse my blemishes, my blackheads, my white heads, my open pores, my irrational combination skin, my uneven skin tone – there could be plenty to find fault with. I spent most of my youth explaining my blemishes to people who least mattered to me (these were mostly staff at the beauty parlour where I had to go every week to get my moustache removed). Inevitably the subject would go to my 'tan' which incidentally happens to be the color of my skin. "You have tanned. Don't you get a facial done?"

Now whichever way you answer this question, you are screwed.

If you say yes, she will go on to elaborate how the previous facial provider had not hydrated your skin enough, or dealt with your whiteheads, or your tan.

If you say no, she will lecture you on the damage the sun and bad products can do to your skin (and by the end of the session would have sold you a 25 gm pot of something the price of a kidney).

I stayed away from facials and such lectures (pretending I had an allergy) and somehow followed my own routine of keeping my skin clean and moisturized, although I did go through a phase of getting swayed by products and a close examination of my dresser was an indicator of my state of mind.

I somehow got bullied into a microdermabrasion (a facial with some dangerous chemicals which costs a bomb) close to my wedding. It was supposed to leave my skin feeling like a baby's skin, instead, left me feeling like a burn victim – I decided I am never letting anyone touch my face again. The bushy moustache and eyebrows still need servicing, so I can't escape that though.

My vanity cupboard has very few products now, compared to the three types of scrubs and serums of my twenties. Ads for wrinkle control and anti-ageing creams flash me by, and nothing happens. I guess I have finally grown into my face.

# 7. In love with love, imaginary relationships, finding 'the one'

I was fifteen when I thought the boy across my building, who came for a walk on his terrace every morning and waved to me – was 'the one'. I stood on my balcony, sipping my coffee, imagining our future together. He was in art school, I loved to write – what a fine couple we would make. May be one day, we could do books together, or start an advertising agency, or maybe I could help him run his studio (I still wasn't sure whether he did Fine Arts or Commercial Art) – we never met enough for me to ask him. And when we did, he was always on his cycle, and I, walking to school or walking back, so it was weird to have a real conversation. Yes, I was still in school, and he – in the big bad world of college.

Later, one day, he sent me a sketch of Jackie Shroff, my ardent crush at the time, one my neighbourhood never got tired of hearing about. Perhaps he heard of it through my brother; they were sort of friends and occasionally played cricket together, although he was much older (the artist, I mean).

When I held the sketch in my hand, and later taped it on behind the door, I thought – this is it. He's the one. Our relationship started having new chapters in my head. Our imaginary relationship, that is.

Of course, none of this was ever spoken about – to him or anyone else, and one day, my family moved homes and that was that.

A few years later – perhaps when I was nineteen and at university and had just become very popular on campus, a tall, lanky boy walked up to my table at the canteen while I was deep in conversation with my friends, pulled up a chair and sat next to me and asked, 'You remember once you had poked a boy in the eye with a pencil in grade 4? I am that boy."

I had never had such a flamboyant opening line used on me before. I knew he was the one.

He made me mixtapes, and left notes for me in my lab, in the library, when I was studying, or sometimes, in the tapes. We went for long walks, talked about life and love, music and Kishore Kumar. He told me he had a girlfriend from high school and was unsure what to do with the relationship, since he was now attracted to me. I sighed.

He never left her for me.

I threw the mixtapes years later, but never forgot him.

There were more mixtape guys. Like the friend whose shoulder I cried on when Mixtape 1 left me all messed up; he gifted me *The Prophet* and other writings of Kahlil Gibran, made me more mixtapes with names of songs in the jacket in his beautiful handwriting, helped me with my symposium slides, wrote me lovely letters during the holidays. He too had a girlfriend back home, although he stayed in the boys' hostel on campus. One day, as we walked to the station as he was dropping me home, he held my hand. I knew something had changed. Could my best friend (who also liked holding my hand) be the one, I wondered?

My imagination started writing a new book.

Later he told me we couldn't possibly be together as we were both very strong-minded. I wondered where that came from.

And then there was Bike Boy 1 and 2 and 3. There's always a jumpstart about a biker relationship – something that switches on in an instant and before you know it, you are already enjoying the romance of the open road, freedom, rebellion, coolness, manliness, adventure, and sexiness. Even though a lot of it is about the ride and not the biker. They make you paint quicker chapters, because everything is a blur.

The problem with breakups is that there seldom is a real one. I mean we all say that we broke up with X or that Y broke up with us or you and M have decided to call off the relationship and remain friends. At least that's common practice. But more often than not, the words 'break up' are never said in a breakup. I wish they were. I wish I knew the finiteness of when a relationship is really over. They usually lie festered in the layers of our relationship, clawing us till one of us finds the courage or sense to move on.

I was then introduced to a suitable boy by my best friend at university; I was 21, he was 23 and heading to the US for a PhD. He was safe, culturally familiar, did the right things, said the right things, my parents loved him. I should have been elated, having been wooed like that, that too by someone my mother approved of. We had a long distance relationship for a year. It was decided that I would apply for a PhD and follow him to the US.

He broke up with me on a letter a year later. I cried for two days. It's not that I was madly in love with him; I just hated being rejected so openly.

Well, this didn't kill me, so I thought it will make me stronger. It didn't.

I was determined to be in love, to be the chosen one. I thought it would fix everything.

I am sure it isn't just me. It's happened to dozens of women I know. We find ways to make emotionally unavailable boys (or at least unavailable to us) attractive: He is a self-confessed recluse. He is too focused on his career. He was dumped royally by his wife/ex girlfriend. He had a hard relationship with his mother. His father was an alcoholic. He is such an idealist that he is having trouble fitting into the real world. He is badly hurt. His ex is a stalker. He is a loner. He just can't commit.

It's just complicated, you tell your friends. But once you fix all the bad parts of his life, and turn him into the man you want him to be, the man he is capable of becoming, your happily ever after will begin. You can feel it in your heart.

Except it is the biggest lie you will tell yourself.

Meanwhile you are busy revisiting your life as if it were a movie screenplay – there are scenes you want to rewrite, dialogues you want to edit, sequencing you want to change – just so you have just the perfect recipe for a real relationship, because right now, it's not going the way you want.

We have all been there: being in 'sort of' relationships with 'sort of' boyfriends who we think 'sort of' love us or at the very least – have things to say to us that they cannot say to anyone else; men who are so complex that you need great powers and unimaginable intuition and radioactive sensors to decode the signs that tell us what we want to hear. We have all drifted along with men without plans, men you have no idea why you are with (even if you are not really 'with' them), men who hit and run, who make a move and then have no idea how to back it up or are unsure whether they really want to. When I look back at how many 'the one' moments I have had in my life, I feel both dizzy and embarrassed. In between all these imaginary relationships there were some real ones that I let materialize: some really nice boyfriends who I felt truly loved and nurtured by, including the man I finally married and made a baby with. But turns out he wasn't 'the one' either, because we are not together any more.

Luckily every woman has an emotional admin, that mirror you need to look into from time to time, that mirror you will often avoid because quite simply – she will call your bullshit and tell you to drop the turd you are into and move on, because seriously, there is nothing there. She will ask you very simple and point blank questions like, "Has he told you he loves you? Or that he really likes you? Has he really put himself out for you?" and you will mumble and fumble and have lots to say about the signs because signs are all you have.

The point is: our imaginary lovers seem to be going through the rest of their life quite breezily without us. Because love is mostly a woman thing: the chase of it, the romanticizing of it. Your market value is judged by whether you are chased and desired by men. And so we make it our greatest mission. It's our desire to get picked, to be the chosen one, to complete another, to get a man to own us, be ours. To eventually win, aka get married. Single women are still considered work in progress and threateningly close to expiry date (my parents thought I was a time bomb ticking away the day I hit 35), while single men are attractive at any age.

We are constantly examining our imaginary love stories in our heads – constructing and deconstructing scenarios – decoding what he said to reveal what he really meant, looking for signs, seeing signs while none exist: in text messages, whatsapps, facebook, instagram, and all the avatars in which it is humanly possible for one person to exist. We feel it's normal, because everyone we know is going through it as well. One-sided love has been glorified in the movies and books, but it's nothing but heartbreak. And pain and emotional disintegration is not a by-product of love. It shouldn't be. Real love, on the other hand, is reciprocative. It's a journey, it's participative. It's never 'sort of', it's finite. And when you are truly in love, there is nothing much to say, nothing to decode, no subtext to read, no signs to interpret. Have you noticed how friends get all quiet once they meet the love of their lives?

If only we put in as much effort into the ones who really care about us, seeing the real signs that exist, the real love stories waiting to happen, the real people who make the move, take the initiative, have a plan – we have no idea what kind of happiness awaits us.

I always believed that if given a chance and nurtured well, friendships will last longer than love. I have been friends with some men for over two decades and it has something to do with the fact that I never ended up having sex with them.

I dated in the pre-Tinder era and got married just before Facebook came to India. That must make me a relic. I never got to left-swipe a guy. The closest I came to being right swiped was when a guy ranked me high in a speed dating event (yes, I went for one of those for a first-person story as a journalist).

But when I look at dating in today's times – when a potential mate has enough opportunity to stalk your (over-curated) life on social media for months before actually asking you out – I thank my stars that at least I got to date (and meet men) organically. Ok, some of them were planted. But still.

I had once tried to simplify men we date in a relationship column I used to write years ago. The theory I came up with was that we date two kinds of men: shampoos and conditioners. The shampoo man pokes your existential dilemmas and all the scabs you are dying to hide, digs out your rough bits, makes you cry, gets all the muck out of you, cleanses you of 'issues' and extraneous stuff, and eventually leaves you to be your free, uncluttered self. The conditioner man smoothens your rough edges, soothes, tames the frizz, nurtures and nourishes you, and stays on to help you ... well, sort of bounce and shine.

Every man wants to be a conditioner, but whether they like it or not, quite a few men have to do the dirty work of being the shampoo. Ideally, what is recommended by experts is a combination of shampoo and conditioner, the sequence in which they appear being of prime importance. Women usually graduate from shampoos to conditioners in men, but sometimes they could end up with a shampoo man, and never know what a conditioner man could have done for them.

The jury is still out on whether one man can be both. For the moment, at least trichologists or hair-care experts will tell you, "Shampoos are supposed to leave and conditioners are supposed to stay. How can they be together?"

Most women have been through more shampoos than conditioners in men and it takes quite a few rinses to know if either of them is doing a good job. But then they say, it's never too late to discover a good hair product. In my experience, the twenties are about shampoos and the thirties are about conditioners. If you are well into your thirties and still haven't graduated from shampoos, you need to take note and figure out why.

It's easy to forget the shampoos once we reach our good hair days, and are basking in conditioners, but we must all remember that it is they who made us what we are. So here's a quick thank you to all the shampoos of my life.

The thing about love, much as we hate to admit it, is that it is constantly directing our life's script – what we do, how we do it, what we feel, what we believe. It's at the forefront of our minds and often our actions. The idea of being unloved, undesired, destroys every woman. It is hard to inoculate oneself against heartbreak, whether one is 20 or 40 or 60. Hearts are strange things – they are as fragile at 50 as they were at 15. We have just become better at camouflaging.

But love holds us back much more than we think it does. It stops us from changing the game, from being spontaneous, from taking that leap of faith, from pursuing that programme on climate change in Costa Rica, from teaching yoga in Rishikesh.

An easy and popular narrative to follow is to love yourself and believe that 'the one' is you. I often wonder: What if you didn't have to wait for that person who completes you? What if you learnt how to do it yourself? I am at a point where I am happy believing that may be I was 'the one' all along, and may be the universe wanted to give me a chance to (finally) fall in love with myself, to win myself as a prize.

Maybe you are your happily ever after. Maybe love is one of those vestigial organs, like the appendix or the male nipple that evolution is training us to live without. And I must say we are getting better at adapting. But the beautiful thing is: each heartbreak leaves a different imprint. Yes, it breaks you, yes it makes you fearful, yet every single time, it makes you want to fly.

# 8. Work. Life. Balance. (or the art of playing office office)

For a long time I have been wondering if I was a job person or a career person. Turns out, I seem to have made a career for myself as a writer while hopping jobs that really didn't mean much to me (except one or two). But every time I hold forth on my career backstory, I find myself making every job on my resume seem relevant. Especially when someone wants to hire me. Even as I narrate it, I start believing that all those impulsive "I quits" had a deeper, meaningful agenda, that I had it all figured out (even though I was chewing my nails on how to pay rent the next month then). But then your life always makes more sense in hindsight and the same goes for your career path.

There was a time when people frowned at my checkered resume that indicated frequent job hopping. Besides, my professional degree as a post-graduate in pharmacy put me in an uncomfortable spot that took a few years shaking out of.

For most of my career, I have been camouflaging my irregularities. I finally wear it as my identity. It is who I am: a Pharmacy major who traipsed through advertising, journalism, animal NGO work, blogging, teaching, a stint at a parenting website, among others. Now that I am off the job market, writing columns and features for newspapers, magazines and anyone who will pay me is more a means to do the actual writing that I want to do. Ironically, my resume, once worrisome, is now looked upon as 'interesting'.

I have never been good with jobs. I am a runaway girl. I have run away from several jobs. I envy people who stick to the same job for 16 years and then reflect back nostalgically on how it moulded them as people. I also feel sorry for them; they will never know the meaning of living on the edge. There are very few times in my life when I have made a graceful and planned exit. My close friend Manjula says that I have done the same with men too, although I always thought it was not I but they who ran.

There is a thing called gratuity in India. It's a rather large sum of money that an organization you work for gives you at the end of a five year period in lieu of your pledged loyalty. Those of you who have clocked in at least five years in a job will know what it means. I always missed it. The longest I clocked in was four years. I attributed it to the Gemini in me who thrived on change. My marriage lasted six, and yes, there was gratuity in the form of my child.

It was my dream to earn gratuity at least once in my lifetime. Both my parents earned it at the end of their 30-35 year old stints at the same job and were eternally grateful. I wanted to feel that sense of gratitude, so I always prayed at the beginning of any job that its relationship status should change to 'In a relationship' soon enough. With most of them, they remained flings, and I got over them faster than I thought.

My threshold for a new job was the same as a new boyfriend: six months. If I lasted six months, I could do a year, and then two years. Everytime I changed my job, it was like a new relationship – I would give it my all and one day, run.

There are three distinct memories of my going to work days: One is when I couldn't wait to get to my office. The other is when I couldn't wait to get home. The third is when I couldn't wait for lunch hour.

I am told that job hopping is the new normal and millennials change as many as four jobs by the time they are 32. Clearly I was born at the wrong time. It was always normal for me to change jobs when I was bored and I feel a bit shortchanged at having been labeled flighty and unfocused. Or perhaps I was just the messenger.

Every time I hopped jobs, I traveled a bit, sometimes holding out as a freelancer long enough for my savings to dry up, before I got in line again for the next one. And the next one. I like to believe that I am no longer in the market for jobs, but I still go for interviews whenever I am summoned, just so I am in touch. Five minutes into the interview, I know what I am not missing and I am grateful to go back home and brew myself a pot of orange tea, as I wonder what to write next. As someone who has spent 20 odd years at various jobs, I think I have earned it.

Here's the thing about work: it should always be satisfying in itself yet leave you happy enough to want to do other things – they could be zentangling or rappelling or spending time with your family. Work is being largely perceived as the means to finding yourself apart from providing you the means to live. *What do you do* is probably the first question a stranger or acquaintance might ask you, as if that is the only way to figure out who you are.

But if your work leaves you angry and takes you further and further away from yourself every single day, you need to take a close hard look at it and find a way out. I never took my job home, and when work people called me after work, it bothered me. It did even when I was a rookie.

There are various things that decide your comfort level in a particular job: the level of air conditioning, the state of the loos, the quality of water cooler conversations, availability of subsidized meals, and sometimes, coupons to buy groceries. Another useful bit of information is whether the company does interesting offsites or if they throw you into the banquet hall of a suburban hotel whose carpets stink.

Of course there are things like the quality of work, job satisfaction, learning curve, the amount of bounce you feel every morning while going to work and the friends you make at work. And that's one more thing to be said about people who change jobs – they make many more friends. Although in the time of Facebook, this may not seem like a big thing, but it is.

Finding the right job is like finding a bra that fits well; it feels just right, yet doesn't remind you constantly that it's a job. One question that I still find difficult to answer honestly in an interview is: So what is it that you really want to do? Well if I really wanted that job, it's hard to answer this. Because what I might really want to do is carpentry. Or move to a country where I can live in a tree house and write while someone pays my bills. That's what I'd like, right? Or I might want to style people – give them different looks, change the way they dress, their hair (I believe every woman is just a haircut and an ensemble away from looking gorgeous). Or that I want to redesign kitchens (again, no experience, but I am sure I can wing it).

When I was in advertising and walked to work (I lived in a working women's hostel then), I used to be one of the first people to show up and naturally wanted to be one of the first people to leave as I always had other interesting things to do after work – like catch a play, a short film or just my dance class. I realised then that people (mostly in advertising) pulled rank by displaying how long they could hold an entire office to ransom before they pulled out their brains for an alleged 'brainstorming'. Three agencies later, I decided that unless I was reporting on national calamities, these timelines just didn't make sense. I then went on to be a journalist and worked for the newspaper and magazine industry, where although the work was far more rewarding (and it had my name on it, yay), the need for face time beyond human ability was still annoying. Your place in the organization was chiefly a reflection of how long you could keep someone waiting for an approval.

Last year, I got rejected for what I thought would be my dream job. It was the first time I found myself saying 'we' effortlessly about an organization, the first time I wanted to be part of something bigger than myself. Unfortunately I don't think they took me seriously when I told them that the job could be my happily ever after.

Office time is a lot about admin. It's about smoke breaks, tea breaks, water cooler breaks, lunch breaks, rinse, repeat. Your career will comprise many such office spaces and each one will add up in an invisible way to who you eventually become (yes, even the jobs you didn't like).

In my earlier job with a film magazine, by the time people got into the work zone, it was usually time to go home. Till today I haven't worked in a single office where I felt most people were optimizing their productivity. I often felt that three hours of working at home made me get a lot more done than 8-10 hours at an office. It was just a pity that people wanted to pay you five times more just for face time. I never understood that. Most of office was to me about playing 'Meeting-meeting'. Or 'let's sit on it'. I guess most people sat on it so much, they got hemorrhoids. Of course if you really like the job, none of this matters, but if you are remotely itchy, then either of these can be triggers to go hunting.

Some say you should work for good people. Some say it's about the organization, never the people. I would always choose people over an organization, because no matter what I do, (even clocking 16 years), the organization will always be bigger than me. Clearly I am not the best person to give career advice. But I can tell you this: always make sure you stay relevant in a way that is unique and sexy. Because the easiest thing to happen when you blend in is that you become irrelevant. And especially watch out for work-life balance when there are major life changes – marriage, divorce, pregnancy, empty nest.

Here are the few things I noticed in my roughly 20 years of working at various jobs:

1. Bosses who display smiley happy family photos always flirt with you.
2. If a boss doesn't want to go home, he/she often resents that you want to.
3. When you gossip in the office loo, someone behind the door is always listening.
4. Smoke breaks (even if you don't smoke) are the best places for gossip because of the poor acoustics.
5. Try and avoid sleeping with your boss if the job is important to you.
6. If your organization is not open to conversations about feminism, it's time to move.
7. There is always someone sleeping with someone. Let it not be your problem.
8. Never trust what anyone says to you at work. The real dope is in your KRA forms.

9. Speaking your mind is not always conducive to a work space.
10. If you spend a great deal of your office hours wondering when you will go home, or a great deal of your home hours wondering when you will go to work, there is something wrong either at office or at home.
11. Leaving before your boss is still considered politically incorrect in some places.
12. Do great work. Someone will notice. That someone could poach you for the next big thing.

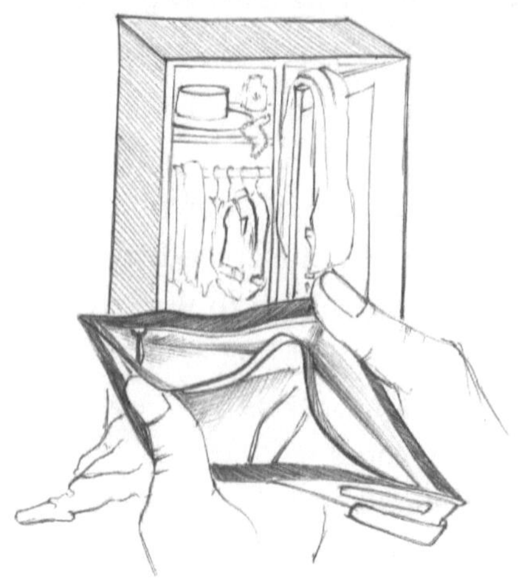

# 9. Money is not a four letter word

Of all the things that don't enter the realm of polite conversation, money figures quite high: talking about it, wanting it, spending it, having it, not having it, having too much or too little. Most of us are brought up to think that talking money is not cool, almost vulgar.

I have also observed that women don't talk about money nearly enough – they are almost apologetic when it comes up in conversation, or plain ignorant. Which explains why they often end up with the short end of the stick in negotiations – whether it's a job, a business, a marriage or a divorce.

"I don't really get money" seems to be an auto response of women for the most part. When I hear smart, otherwise successful women say this, it bothers me. Especially when they say it as though it's a fashion statement. That's like taking pride in not knowing basic shit.

Money is basic. It will be the only constant in your life, and will keep coming up for a dialogue with you. So if you don't know it enough, now is not a bad time to start.

We learn a lot from each other about relationships or work, but we seldom learn (or even ask questions) about money. I have always had friends who I knew were doomed as far as money was concerned, and when I watched them be foolish with it, I offered my two bits, whether they liked it or not.

I have some news for you ladies: Being a mess is no longer exotic or cute. Being a financial mess – even less so. It is one thing to be ignorant about money and it's quite another for this ignorance to be compounded by diseases of the retail kind. We can't be Carrie Bradshaws buying Manolo Blahniks despite not being able to make rent. It's not easy finding a sugar daddy to pay our rent or buy our apartment for us. That's not cute at 20, and most certainly not at 40. Life is not *Sex and the City*. Wearing your chaotic, reckless, money-ignorant self on your sleeve is not cool. Neither is not knowing how to negotiate salaries, plan investments or file taxes. It's basic shit, and you better start now if you aren't good at it.

It's a sad truth that we often learn about money through circumstance, but I think finance and economics should be taught in school at an early stage. I learnt about money the hard way too, mostly through adversity and especially because 50% of my gene pool has always had a problematic relationship with money (and still does). Growing up, I had a father, who, although had a regular job, always lived hand to mouth. Like sometimes, we would go on vacations and run out of money on our return trip (yes). He also was a bad judge of character and was constantly putting his money where his mouth was (read: in get-rich-quick schemes that backfired). Thank god my mother worked too, and her income was always the more dependable one, because left to my father, we would have defaulted on school fee payments most of the time.

One of the turning points in my life was when my father was bankrupt and without a job, and my mother had her first heart attack – she had to be operated immediately for a valve replacement. I could envision that my mother may not be able to return to work, and that we could not depend on my father for financial support. I was then the only other earning member of my family (my brother had just started his career as a software engineer). But more than paying the medical bills, there was the larger question of where we would live once my mother left her job (we were then living in the staff quarters of her company).

And so, with much trepidation and in a market that was booming, I made my first real estate decision – and quietly filled a loan application. That 1 BHK and my subsequent commitment to a Rs 3300 EMI towards it at a time when I was unsure which way I wanted my career to go – was the bravest thing I ever did. I was signing my first home sale deed at the age of 27. My family of course was in denial that I could wing it. I guess I was raised to believe that I would grow up, get married and be looked after, so looking after my family was never part of the plan.

When I got my first job as an advertising trainee, I managed to save something every month even on my Rs 1700 per month stipend. As the years passed and my income grew, I did go through a phase where I was spending a lot on the usual things girls spend money on – clothes, shoes, bags, accessories. It was obvious I was desperately striving to be a better version of myself. It never helped.

The problem with this kind of spending is that it is actually more likely to bring you back a step, and make you feel even worse. Your growth as a person isn't consistent with how much you spend on clothes or supplies or how many LBDs you have. Because we are constantly opening our closets and looking for those items missing that will turn us into the truly fabulous people we want to believe we are. It's a trap. You will always be one jacket, one saree, one piece of jewelry, one stole, one dress away from gorgeousness.

The day you open your closet and tell yourself: "I am enough" and know that even if you bought no clothes or shoes for a year, you could still look good is the day you turn into a real grown-up in control of her finances. There will also be a day when I feel capable of completing my daily tasks without having the most perfect planner or Bullet Journal to write my to-do list in.

One of the issues with my marriage was that we had entirely different relationships with money. His was abusive, mine was nurturing. The single most liberating thought when I decided to walk away was – I don't have to carry on because I am strong enough financially to do life on my own. The one thing money (or knowing and understanding it) did for me is: I always felt empowered to make life-changing decisions – like changing a job or career, taking a gap year, writing a book, walking out of my marriage. I had seen enough women suffer through bad marriages because when they did the math, they realised they couldn't afford the lifestyle they were living. And somehow divorces never resulted in settlements that are talked about in celebrity marriages. Instead they made the woman realise she had nothing to her name, plus now she had two children to look after and no child support to speak of, so she has to put herself right back in the job market.

For the benefit of all of you who are trying to have a better relationship with money, here is a list of 16 money rules I put together. They may seem pretty basic, but it is shocking how ignorant women are even on the basics.

### 1. Balancing your accounts

This simply means balancing what you earn against what you owe (and spend) and making sure your credit always exceeds your debit. The way to do this is to list down all your expenses and all your income and add them up. If your expenses exceed your income, something is surely off and you need to find a way to reduce your debt. This is particularly good for those of us who refrain from writing accounts because we are scared what they may reveal. It helps when you know how much money you have in reserve and what is available to spend.

### 2. Credit card 101

First things first: A credit card is not money you have. It's money you owe. And you must know that this money will keep growing exponentially by a stealthy device called compound interest (which is actually interest on interest and just to give you a rough idea: it is twice that of a home loan). So if you only pay what is the minimum amount owed on your credit card every month, you are going to be in huge debt very soon. Are you the type who cannot recall what you spent on that had incurred you a huge credit card bill? Are you using your credit card for things you cannot afford otherwise? Do you feel that your credit limit is actually your bank balance? Do you find yourself applying for a new card when all your credit cards are maxed out? Then you need some serious credit card therapy.

### 3. Shopaholics anonymous

Shopping is the most expensive way to feel good, and there's a reason they call it retail therapy. Imagine giving so much power to clothes and shoes as a means of feeling good. It is an addiction, like any other and to get over it, you need to divert the urge somewhere else, take occasional inventories of things you own and never wear and most importantly: try to distinguish between want and need. A friend of mine suggested a small tip which always works for me: The next time you go shopping, wear your coolest clothes that make you feel super attractive. The urge to shop is much less.

### 4. Having a goal. Sticking to it.

Formulate a plan with a goal for a month, six months or a year and chart your progress as you move along. I usually promise myself an incentive like a holiday or a piece of luggage or home improvement. At the end of it, you will experience the joy of earning your own reward.

### 5. Having spend-free days

Try a day in a month where you carry no money or cards and see how it goes. Walk, carry lunch that day, and try and observe where the urge to spend money strikes you the most. The experience will make you richer. The early days of demonetization in November 2016 was a reality check for me. I realised how much money I spent mindlessly, even though I don't use credit cards.

### 6. Investing well

Instead of avoiding sections in newspapers that talk money, try reading up on investments and spread your money over some regular old-fashioned schemes like PPF and post office savings as well as newer ones like mutual funds. There are books and columns on money management. You can set aside a small amount every month and track it and slowly raise the bar. Stocks and real estate are other options, but it requires a deeper understanding of the market. But nothing is rocket science really.

### 7. Rewarding yourself

Treat yourself to small pleasures whenever you have been good with money: some nice dessert, books, fresh flowers, scented candles, a spa treatment.

### 8. Giving back to the community

Once you have been good with money for a while, start donating for a cause you believe in and something you can track. It will create a feeling of abundance and joy that shopping can never match.

### 9. Planning your retirement

You need to have a nest egg both as assets and savings for your retirement irrespective of a spouse or lack thereof or whether your parents are going to leave you a nice inheritance. You will also have to factor in that you will still need money for your expenses long after you stop earning and you don't want to be dependent on children/family. You will be surprised how few women factor this in. I have already budgeted for a halfway house with my friends when I am 60. I don't believe children should be treated as old-age insurance.

### 10. Knowing your net worth

It is important to have a rough idea of how much your assets, savings, investments are worth and what they total up to, so you always have a realistic image of what you have at your disposal, in case of an emergency. Another thing is to ensure that there are a few things in your name (you have no idea how many women are clueless about this) so that you know you are never down to zero just because you chose to walk out on a marriage. Divorce battles are long and tedious, especially when money is involved, so make sure you don't end up on the short end of the stick.

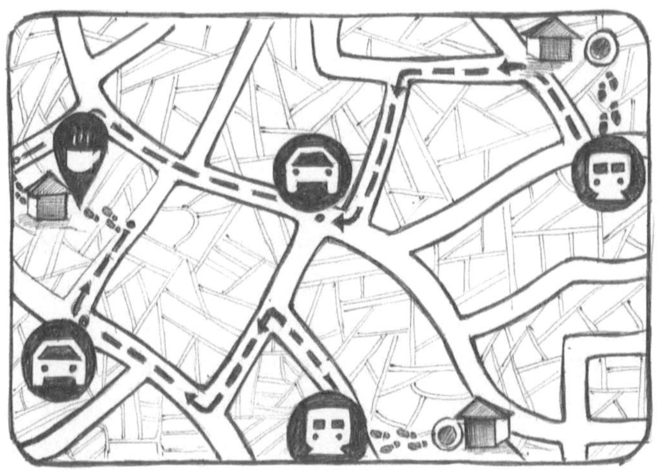

# 10. Friends and the art of showing up

Every month, my mother and her two besties have a chat on the phone which goes like this:

Are you there?

Yes, yes, where will I go?

I am coming.

Come, come.

And then one of them changes buses and trains for two hours to show up at the other's home, catch up on all that happened during the month, have a meal, exchange some food goodies (usually a pickle, a chutney or some such) and makes her way back. Sometimes they have a sleepover and giggle through the night. They are all 70 plus and have undergone multiple surgeries and been advised by their doctors not to strain or travel much.

But friendship has no rules. When you gotta go, you gotta go. At least that's how it used to be. Keeping in touch with friends is as uncomplicated as that. You make a plan, you show up.

For the longest time, it's been our friendships with other women that has allowed us to become who we truly are, as opposed to say, marriage or family. Our friends complete us in pretty much the same way as a soulmate does. When relationships are depleting, it's friendships we turn to for replenishment, connection, a shared sensibility and laughs. Our women friends also help us raise the bar; we look up to our friends more often and in more ways than we think. And with the transience of marriage and relationships, it is often our female friends who do the job of spouses, and are often better at it. How many times have you told a female friend, "You know, I should have so married you!"

Every straight girl has at some point wished she were a lesbian, because her women friends really 'got' her much more than men. The bonds we form with each other are deeper and last longer than we give them credit for. Women often find in friends what they may never find in love.

For most women, friendships are the constants in their life; they see them through breakups, moving homes, bad relationships, family issues, illnesses and divorce.

As more women marry later in their lives, we find more time to be ourselves with our female friends, and find a long enough window to nurture our friendships, often almost a decade or longer, while we wait for the suitable men to show up. We lean in for each other, we urge each other to be stronger, sharper, better versions of ourselves, we encourage each other to make healthy choices, we dissuade each other from settling for anything less than what we are worthy of.

In general, women have always had higher benchmarks in friendship compared to our male counterparts. Men can form friendships simply on the basis of activity – playing pool, watching soccer, drinking beer. For women, the transition from acquaintance to friend takes a while, that from friend to close friend, or someone that forms part of your inner circle takes even longer.

Men on the other hand, don't share much; they never really allow that degree of access to friends, and besides, they don't particularly like answering questions. Most men have 'best friends' who don't know their secrets – but it doesn't matter – there is not much emotion invested, and hence no major disappointments. If you do friendship like a man, you are less likely to get hurt.

I once dated a guy who was constantly having random strangers over and cooking for them. He said he worked on the law of probability. That if he invited 25 strangers (usually friends of friends, but not necessarily), his ROI on it would be at least one or two new friends he would want to keep. And that, to him was not bad Math, as opposed to going clubbing, spending a few thousands in one night and barely being able to make any conversation, leave alone making a friend.

I found his approach very endearing in a space where people were only doing things that were convenient for them. His parties always had a great turnout because there was always good food, you always met new people (and it was amazing how he kept it going).

Female friendships rely heavily on consistency, on the frequent updates, the all-knowingness, and this becomes harder when we have to invest ourselves intensely in say, a marriage or a relationship that can take a lot out of us. The divides between women friends can creep in just as they do in marriages. Friendships can hurt too, and at 48, I still find myself having sleepless nights over a thoughtless, casual remark from a friend or a text message that seemed too breezy for its own good.

Friendship is not always convenient. It is the most inconvenient thing to show up. But you do it. Friendships are all-consuming too. When you offer your loyalty and your time to a friendship, you expect the same in return. I used to be good at friendship. I was good at showing up; I was also consistent. I was the friend someone cried on when they were going through man trouble. I was the friend who they called when they wanted to buy Duckback raincoats and didn't know where to go. I remembered birthdays, I used to be an expert on break-up food, I knew what a new mother wanted, I never complained that any place was 'too far' to visit and I was happy to cook for (and be fed by) people.

And then I think Facebook happened, and we all began to hug the illusion of having more friends than we ever really had. I am struggling with friendships now that I have so many 'friends'. I am struggling with choosing who to be my real self with. My vulnerability is losing practice, so much so that I now see a therapist and keep a journal just to stay in touch with my authentic self.

Now I have to keep track of friends' newsfeeds on Facebook, because people don't call and tell you things anymore. And you think, maybe this is the way to do it, and you do it for a while and then you feel quite weird. It's like we are so preoccupied with how we look and sound on social media, that we have forgotten how we really look and sound. We have become a version of ourselves. And that version has started believing in 'likes' and other algorithms of friendship.

One thing that bothered me about the man I married is that he had no real, steady friends and he even said so. He attributed it to having led a nomadic life, having lived abroad for the first 25 years of his life, never in the same country for more than three years. Which is why, whenever there was talk of inviting people over, and we were down to a list, he would say, "Let's invite four or five extras in case people don't show up." I was amused. "If you are a friend, you show up," I would say. It was not how it worked for him.

In the first few years of our marriage, we hosted brunches and dinners almost every weekend at our small flat with a big heart. I wanted to make a point of yours+mine =ours and fill my house with conversations and love; I wanted to celebrate what brought us together. After a few years, I noticed that there were no return invitations. Not that I was banking on it, but it would have been nice if people had extended us the same hospitality to us that we did them. Instead, we got bulk texts to attend birthday parties of 40-year-olds where you had to pay for your drinks and buy your own food.

## FRIENDSHIP METER: BUMP ALERT

Consistency is a tricky thing about friendship, and we need to constantly redefine our *friends forever* romanticism. Every friendship goes through trying times; some make it stronger, and some make you realise that it is no longer worth holding on. In any case, we all need to do a regular housekeeping on friendships and sometimes it might be worth letting some friendships go if you aren't able to nurture them. Here are 13 ways to test a friendship:

### 1. When one of you is a constant whinebag

If you are constantly using a friend as a sounding board, you are going to deplete her at some point. It is very tempting to use that one friend to rant and rave all the time, but take a walk, make yourself a cup of tea and ask yourself: do you still want to make that call to whine?

### 2. When you can't count on your friend

Being dependable is one of the strongest qualifications for friendship. If you are a constant slacker – never show up on time, never bring the chips or wine you were supposed to bring to the party, never return calls or messages on time – very soon your friends are going to give up on you. I have dropped friends I couldn't count on after a few incidents of general slackness.

### 3. When there is constant rivalry

We have always had work buddies at some point, but it's important to keep track of when work and friendship are constantly bleeding into each other too aggressively. Find ways to focus things that you share outside of work, ask yourself what is the real basis of your friendship.

### 4. When one of you cannot deal with the other's success

True friends stick by you through your ups and downs, but remember to show a little sensitivity when you've landed that dream job and are constantly flying to Vienna and Paris while your friends are still dealing with school pickups and PTAs and can't cope with the exclamation points in your status messages.

### 5. When distance is a deterrent

Now with facebook and other social media, keeping track of what your friends are upto is no longer a problem, but it is not a substitute for a real connection once in a while – either in person, or on skype, a phone call or just good old email.

### 6. Money

It is not the easiest thing coping with a friend who has suddenly run into money (she has got VC funding, signed a movie or has married rich) and suddenly, doing 'normal' things like grabbing a drink or street side shopping seem off the list. Instead you are meeting for cocktails you can't really afford at expensive bars.

## 7. Change

Sometimes we make sudden life changes – like stop drinking or turn vegan or get into a strange diet and our friends cannot cope. Motherhood also makes us very extreme in our views for a bit and wearing it on our sleeves is detrimental to our friendships. Sometimes we really need to decide how much we value old friendships and how much of it are we prepared to salvage despite all the changes in our life. We all change as individuals and often grow apart; but parting because of it is unnecessary.

## 8. Traveling with a friend

One thing I am very wary of is holidaying with friends. When you share a room together and are locked in for a week of travel, it is something that reveals the true personality of the said friend and you may have to deal with things you never had to before. I have lost two friends (at different times) post traveling with them, so be very careful who you choose who you travel with. Especially when you have kids (or husbands, or both, because it just makes the variables much more complicated and layered).

## 9. Favours

Always keep a track of things that you ask a friend to do for you and check if you are returning favours adequately. If she babysat your kid, offer to take hers out one day for a movie. If she returned your library books, offer to pick up books for her another time. If she fed you a nice meal, call her over for lunch one day. If you receive, you must give in equal measure.

## 10. Betrayal

In this treacherous world of 'mutual friends' cropping into every friendship, one needs to be constantly careful about spilling salacious details about one friend's life to another; it only goes to show that you cannot be trusted and that you thrive on juicy gossip. Of course everyone loves gossip, but it's good to set some boundaries of things you will never discuss about another person in their absence. Because word gets around and it is still a very small world and remember, you have 47 mutual friends. Something's gotta give.

### 11. Boredom

If you are constantly doing the same friend things together – meeting at the salon, shopping, watching a movie, it is quite easy to slip into boredom out of repetitive acts when you are never really discovering new things about each other. How about taking a sourdough bread making class or starting a book club. Basically, change the game. I would say the same thing for relationships too.

### 12. Taking friends for granted

Sometimes, you may take a joke too far or pull one too many scabs and cause a friend to clam up. It's important to always know and respect your boundaries.

### 13. Constant role playing

It's important to change friendship dynamics once in a while. If you are the constant host and provider of advice and food, put your feet up once in a while and act needy. If you are constantly problem solving for the other, giving advice, act helpless and seek answers too.

## THE ART OF MAKING NEW FRIENDS

When I figured at some point that most of my close friends were not in my city any more, I ended up building some really meaningful friendships with a few 'facebook friends'. Whenever I like someone from the virtual world, I want to make it real quickly. I have even travelled cities and countries to meet people who I thought had friendship potential. That's just how I work.

Once, I had this 'friend' on social media who I had started to like and she liked me back too, but every time I was in her city (and that year I travelled a lot), and would offer to meet her, she would go silent. Until I asked, "How come you don't feel like meeting me?"

She was taken aback, as if I had violated some sacred online code and said, "But I am liking, sharing, so we are connected no?"

Then there are the ones who will find out (of course from facebook or instagram) that you are in their city, and they will message you: *Hey, I heard you were in Goa! We must meet up when you are here next.*

At which you say: *Why next, I am here now. Where do you live?*

*Oh, it's really far from where you are at.*

*That's okay. How far?*

*An hour. Let's just meet on the beach, because I really want to get out of home, and so do my boys.*

And with that, she excused herself from having to extend an invitation to her home. In any case, home is no longer where the heart is for most people. People are not inviting people home anymore, because your home is who you are, and no one wants to share that. It's becoming easier to live in people's minds as a version of your last selfie. Not that I was expecting a four course meal or spa services at her house. But I find it odd when people always deflect you from their homes and yet keep insisting you have to meet.

And then you also lose friends.

I also lost some because they got too busy with their marriage and couldn't wait for me to catch up.

I lost some because they were too busy with their kids.

I lost some because their marriages ended and I was forced to pick a side.

I lost some to my fertility. I begat a child when they were struggling with their wombs.

I lost some because they didn't approve of the man I married.

I lost some because they didn't approve that I gave up on my marriage.

And then there are friends who suddenly go cold on you. Like, stone cold. They stop responding to texts, messages, they are busy climbing other walls and timelines and ignoring you, and you wonder, was it something I did? They don't reply.

I now know that it's called ghosting.

I don't know why this happens. What I do know is that friendship often requires an ecosystem of shared grief, shared passion, shared happiness or something that brought the two of you together. Very often, you just outgrow friends or you lose the thing that brought you together. For the longest time, I was the singleton with man troubles and I was this very easy person for married friends to adopt (oh, let's sort you out) or other angry single friends (yes, it really sucks). When I moved to the other side, got married and had a baby, I suddenly became the one who had jumped ahead in the race. I must say I lost a few friends there. Clearly the ones who dropped off were not the ones for the long haul, but it hurt anyway. I wish there was a civilized way to break up with a friend, like you do in a romantic relationship; I wish people wouldn't just slink away and hide behind 'workload', bad marriages, grumpy husbands or kids. I have lost (and have been ghosted by) a few friends and sometimes I have been the dumper too; I only wish there was a more formal way to do it.

Then there are the 'let's meet up, let's do lunch, let's hang out' types. I have a quick detection programme for such scammers. I set a date. "How about Tuesday?" I ask. It's enough to sift the ones who really want to do the work from those that have no intention whatsoever and could spend the rest of their life 'liking' your posts on facebook, but never really wanting to meet you. For the former, I'd do anything. Cook up a storm, negotiate downpours, drive on second gear, climb potholes, anything. And they would return the favour in ample measure.

And like my friend Jo pointed out: the real cement is kindness, especially when you have kids. It lasts much longer than 'connection'. So it's no longer about 'People Like Us', but people who care enough to show up.

These days I find it a lot easier to become friends with rank strangers because you never have to worry about your backstories. I may have made a few wrong calculations in this, but it was still worthwhile.

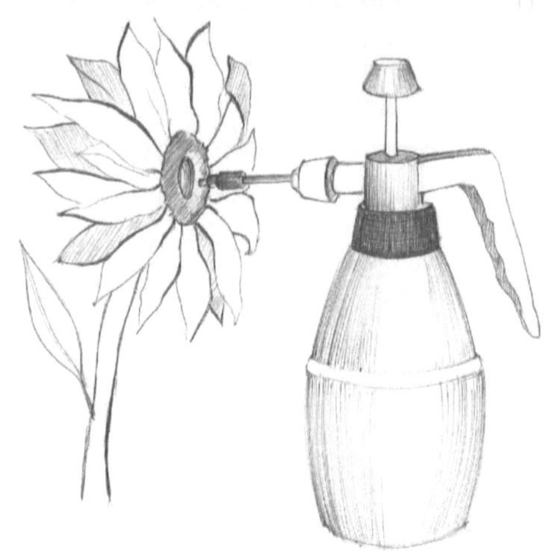

# 11. Between the covers: things they don't tell you about sex

It is a truth universally unacknowledged that every girl in possession of a hymen is looking for a deflowering agent.

It's another truth no one talks about that losing your virginity to said agent is the most unspectacular event of your life.

Forget all the 'first time' stories you have heard so far. They were all lies, because no one tells you the real truth; not even your BFF. What you hear is a romanticised, thoroughly fictionalized, filtered 15 second edit of it. Losing your virginity is the most un-memorable detail of your sex life, one that you want erased from your memory as soon as you start getting some real action. No one wants to talk about the first time. It is really bad copy.

First of all, a large part of the 'first time' (or even many times later) is spent finding the hole (you and the person you are trying to have sex with). And since penetration has always been sold as the defining moment in sex (something that you take several years of bad sex to unlearn), we spend years (that we could otherwise have in pleasure giving and receiving) merely in locating said hole so that said object of affection's penis might make its way into it.

So much for 'saving it for that special guy'.

Most of early sex is clumsy, fidgety, awkward, abandoned halfway and either spent in self-pleasing, or, if the company is really good – talking or watching a film.

The deflowering agent is a job no one really wants. Because no one wants to be the first one to go where no man has gone before. It must be a terrible job – messy, exhausting, frustrating and not at all rewarding.

I always wondered how it works for childhood sweethearts where there is nowhere else to go and they only end up having sex with each other for the rest of their lives (because of course they get married and want to live happily ever after).

The 'first time' is the most overrated event in the entire universe and what spoils it for most of us is we believe all these 'magical' stories. The fact that there is a unique penis in this world meant only for your vagina, and once the twain meet, it's the greatest love story ever.

What a load of cock! (sorry, I couldn't help that).

My advice to all girls is to lose their virginity as quickly and uneventfully as possible, so that your body is ready for the real, exciting sex you are about to have with all the wrong and not-so-wrong guys in the world.

Everyone has their (untold) first time story. Here is mine: I lost my virginity to a clinic.

I was a late bloomer in the sex department too. After years of unsuitable men abandoning ship, because they were daunted by the idea of deflowering a virgin (I was still one at 24), I decided this was not a blot I wanted to live with. So one day, after a few failed attempts at having sex with this not-so-hot guy I was interested in, I made an appointment with an ob-gyn and told her about my difficult hymen. "I want my hymen to be torn. Can you do that please? Surgically?"

She asked me, "Are you married?" (Perhaps referring to the obligatory sex one has to have after marriage or perhaps judging me for wanting to have premarital sex).

I said no, marriage is far off, but I would like to 'enjoy' for now, and my tight hymen was getting in the way of spontaneity.

She then anesthetized me and performed a little thing. When I came to, I was deflowered. She also told me she hadn't ruptured it entirely and had left a bit of it, so that the man would have the 'satisfaction'. I was angry with her and almost wanted my money back when I realised it was actually far more okay than where I was.

Yay! I called the guy I was dating then, and told him I was ready.

He sounded nervous and said he'll call me back. He never did, but it didn't matter because now I was free and available to the rest of the world. I could have wild, spontaneous sex with whoever I wanted.

Here is what I feel: If you find a guy remotely interesting, and would consider a relationship with him, get the sex out of the way as soon as you can. We were all conditioned to play hard to get and wait for commitment and all that balderdash, but thank god for Tinder changing the rules of the dating game. Third date is way too late. I feel it's totally okay to have sex on the first date if possible, because it's one thing out of the way, and then the real relationship, if any, has space to grow.

Honestly, what is the point of 'vibing' mentally, if you are not in sync in the sack? Its high time we rewrite the rules of dating and make it mandatory to have sex as early as possible; it just makes it more black and white. Else we will always spend the rest of our lives 'settling' for average or less than average sex with someone we thought we got along with so well. And never be able to tell them that.

I am no expert on sex, but it's been over two decades post losing my virginity and along the way I have had some good and bad sex, and I think I can make some fair generalisations. Here they are, in no particular order:

### Fact 1

If you are using the movies to set up your sex scene (and we all have a favorite one), you will almost always be disappointed. Sex in real life is not the mood-lit, step-wise disrobing, heaving like synchronized swimmers, coming in unison and the pillow talk thereafter. It is very fidgety, always awkward, often lazy and never seamless and what you see in the movies is a perfectly edited, fake version of what really happened (or didn't happen). Watching porn is another level of unrealism which I will come to later.

### Fact 2

There is a huge amount of interest and speculation about singleton sex – because it is exciting, variable, unpredictable and has to be plotted and choreographed: who to have it with, and where to have it. Unless, of course you have a place/room of your own and you have steady access to your boyfriend/ girlfriend/person to have sex with. But most of the world is not so fortunate and spends an inordinate amount of time and effort, planning dirty weekends to Aksa beach, where now, there is also the possibility of getting arrested.

### Fact 3

Married people don't have more sex. Even if they are happily married (and more about that oxymoron in another essay). They just have more access to sex (to the same person every day of course). They have more obligatory sex. Which is: Here is a man/woman lying next to me, and I'm horny and I cannot have Scarlett Johannson/George Clooney, so let me just have sex with this person and go to sleep, because well, we are married and there is nowhere else to go.

### Fact 4

Blowjobs are the biggest scam. No one enjoys giving blowjobs, or being choreographed while doing so. You just do it so that the other party returns the favor, which is great. But every time a woman (and you will always find someone in your hostel, college, workspace) tells you she "loves to give blowjobs", blow her head off. She is making it difficult for the rest of you.

### Fact 5

Wearing a condom doesn't come easily to men and they will make all kinds of excuses – that they are allergic to the rubber, that it hurts, that they are unable to keep their erection once in it. Eight out of ten men will refuse to wear it, pretending to be aghast that you even suggested it, and will suggest things like coming on your breasts or pulling out or some such. If you don't trust their dexterity, you will have to have the condom/birth control talk before you take your clothes off. The onus is largely on you, whether it comes to contraception or even safeguarding against STDs, I would say test yourself regularly, because I can't say choose your partners well; it is a demand-supply situation.

### Fact 6

Not many men like women on top, although it's great for the women. They will pretend they like strong, empowered women, but as soon as you take the power in your hands (and it's easier to control your orgasm when you are on top), they will feel emasculated and find a way to pin you down. So if you like staying on top, say so.

### Fact 7

Having the birth control talk is more awkward than it's made out to be. It also implies that you are assuming it is long term, before such a talk actually happens (and it's never a talk really, it's more an ultimatum).

### Fact 8

There will always be that one friend who wears her sex life on her sleeve and she will always make you feel inadequate. She will also tell you that she loves giving blow jobs to her boyfriend and that they have 'done it everywhere' and that her boyfriend never has a problem with the condom. Screw her!

### Fact 9

For all their non-communication and grunts otherwise, men surprisingly talk a lot during sex, like they've just been struck by a bout of verbal diarrhoea when in bed. Personally, I feel talking during sex is a waste of time unless he is asking you where your clit is. Once a guy got on top of me and demanded, 'Say nice things!' I was so blown that I was speechless and couldn't think of a single nice thing to say. I mostly like my men to shut the fuck up, although they will ask you to 'talk dirty' in that 'who's your daddy' voice and it's always annoying unless you are very drunk. The funny thing is when a man starts choreographing the sex as if it is one big dance and you are like, 'I prefer solos'.

It's totally okay to switch off and use this time to make job lists or plan what to wear to work tomorrow.

### Fact 10

If you are particular about body odor, oral hygiene, clean arm pits, spruced up genitals, it is important to have the talk early on in the relationship. You can't just grin and bear it for years and suddenly find his breath a turn off.

### Fact 11

Hair is an intrinsic part of our genitals, so let us not pretend to have baby-skin out there. When a man expects you to go Brazilian on your pubis, ask him to mow his lawn too. It's totally okay to wax your vulva, but let it not be a thing you *have to* do.

### Fact 12

Skill levels never match during sex, even if you have been married to the same person for 30 years. Remember that three-legged race in school, where the two of you have to be perfectly in sync? Doesn't happen in bed.

### Fact 13

Of course married couples will tell you that sex is great. Because what else can they say?

### Fact 14

It is easier and faster to get off on your own, but it is something unsaid when things are hot and heavy. Watching men get off is not fun, although they will sell it to you as the greatest show on earth ever.

### Fact 15

Sometimes it's better to lie on your back and think of Robery Downey Jr. or Bradley Cooper.

### Fact 16

Penetrative sex is over-marketed, thanks to the movies and almost never results in an orgasm for you, so it is only one-sided. Everything hurts in penetrative sex. Especially if you are not doing yoga, running, swimming or gymming. Most of the ooohs and the aaahs are from your body hurting, not the orgasm.

### Fact 17

You never 'come' together. Almost never ever. What they show in the movies is improbable. Also, and this is true for me: once you have reached orgasm, you do lose interest (I often have to remind myself that there are a lot of obligatory sex operations to be performed) and the rest of the sex is faked passion.

### Fact 18

The vaginal orgasm is extinct. No one I know has it. It's all about the clit. The only reason men want to get in is because it's good for them. It's never about you.

### Fact 19

If he doesn't have the looks, he has the moves, so do consider having sex with that kind ugly guy. He may be able to please you unlike all those good looking blokes you ran after. And in any case sex is about talking your face away, right?

### Fact 20

If you saw your lover's orgasm face in real life, you would probably never sleep with them. They are always weird. Best not to have a mirror around, although some men love it.

### Fact 21

Dear men. Stay away from our vaginas unless we are making babies. You really don't have to enter. All the pleasure is outside. And please get some clit education so that you are not mechanically rubbing in the general area for 15 minutes before you start thrusting excitedly all over again in some silly tribal dance moves.

### Fact 22

Most men need a map for the cervix and the clitoris. They mistake one for the other and sometimes there is a lot of unnecessary poking.

### Fact 23

That woman making orgasmic sounds while he is thrusting? Well they are fake too. There is no way she is coming while he is inside.

I have probably had two vaginal orgasms in my entire life and I remember them clearly. They were the exception and I am not stupid to make them the rule.

### Fact 24

Size does NOT matter. Every man thinks he has the largest dick. Men will keep asking you what you like, and they are waiting for answers which relate to the size of their cock and how much you love sucking on it or shoving it into your mouth, but the fact is, that you'd rather they use their fingers better.

### Fact 25

Watching porn doesn't make you better at sex. It just creates unrealistic expectations and gives false impressions that what you are doing is right. Instead of watching porn, watch a woman pleasing herself. No one likes being whipped, tied, beaten, and have cum being sprayed on their faces.

### Fact 26

Most orgasms are fake. If we scream or moan, or call your name wildly, it's because we think that's what you like us to do. And we also do it so that you can do your job better, which most of the time, you can't and we are so tired, so we just moan as we think of George Clooney.

# 12. The thing about marriage

I spent 38 years of my life single. It was routine for people (usually family members) to ask me at every wedding I attended (and there were so many): "So when are you going to settle down?"

After a long stint at being the best girl at friend's weddings, shopping for maternity clothes with them, holding their hand post-partum, watching them nurse their babies, watching the babies blow their candles, watching their husbands making eyes at other women, I finally made my peace with the situation.

But every time I was asked about my ambivalent status, I found it annoying. Why was marriage the default setting?

If the kind of marriages I saw in my family were 'settling', I was so glad to be unsettled. One day, single will be the new married, I thought.

I am not a cynic. I spent most of my youth chasing love and believing 'this was the one' every time I was loved back. And finally, in my 39th year, after the world and my mother had given up on me, I tied the knot. It happened when it didn't matter whether or not it happened. I was, at that point, having the greatest love affair of my life – the one with myself. Yes, I am gorgeous, but it took me a long time and many wrong guys to fall in love with myself. When I finally did, along came 'the one'.

I found many shallow reasons to write him off. The fact that he looked too young (I thought at that point that he was the younger sibling of the girl who introduced us). The fact that he had an American accent (diplobrat = American schools = funny, mixed up accent of no fixed address). The fact that he couldn't cook. The fact that he couldn't remember the last book he read. The fact that he had never watched a play. The fact that he didn't play any real sport.

And then I found one solid reason not to. The fact that he totally got me. The fact that he made me laugh. The fact that he celebrated me.

We were married a year and a half after we started dating.

From being the 'poor thing' at weddings, I had now acquired an elevated status.

I preferred marriage to dating, frankly. When you are dating, there is all this pressure of being good, putting yourself in the other person's shoes, being sensitive, putting his interest before yours, etc. You also end up doing a lot of things you don't want to do, out of sheer politeness. When the husband and I were dating, it was always about, "Honey, would you like to <insert activity that gives you a rash here>?" And I was like, "Sure, when would you like to go?"

Post marriage, there's freedom. Freedom to say no. Freedom to veto. Freedom to express your views about their life, their friends, their idea of a good time. Freedom to give a rat's ass.

Among other things, marriage was designed to be liberating. After years of the unbearable politeness and syrupy sweetness of dating, marriage was suddenly the freedom to be rude. Order what the hell you want, be as bad as you want, say what you want and never say what you don't want, and all will still be well. I figured we had our whole life to make up, and neither of us was going anywhere. Enough of being polite, letting the other person have their point of view, their thing on the menu, their choice of temperature for air-conditioning, their choice of which place to go to, or who to make brunch plans with.

One of the first things I announced post marriage was that I hated air conditioning. This, after months of negotiating optimum temperatures during our dating phase, which went like:

*Honey, is 20 ok for you?*

*Ummm, may be 23?*

*How about 22?*

*Ok, done!*

Our marriage often reminded me of a scene from *Rules of Engagement* (a popular soap about coupledom), in which Jeff tells Audrey: *You can't be mad at anyone in the world except for me. There's no risk in yelling at me, because, legally, I have to love you.*

For someone who had been single for so long, marriage and its motions were amusing to begin with, and eventually cramping. While love is about newness, liberating and adventure-seeking, marriage is about sameness, and finding joy in it.

This is why I thought marriage was like having a cat:

- Just because we are in the same room, it doesn't mean we have to talk. I know all that talk about nurturing, but silence is good enough.

- Sometimes I might lick you, or give you a pedicure, even if you don't ask for it. It's how I show my love, even though I am not expected to. But don't expect it at the same time, every day. That's what dogs do.
- We have just signed up to be together for life. Can we cut through the crap of 'I love you' and 'You are the most important person in my life' and 'I don't think I can live without you'. Maybe you can say it but I can't. I am a cat.
- It's fine, we are husband-wife, but each one of us is still entitled to the best spot in the bed. The only thing that matters is, who gets there first.
- We are so over the phase of being polite and entertaining random people and doing things to please others. Don't go there.
- Sometimes, I may want to cuddle with you. At other times, I may not feel like showing up when you walk in that door. It should be cool either way.
- I may do things that are out of character, like fetch a ball, or serve you your newspaper in bed, but don't get used to it.
- When you leave town, I get to be me. I love it. So don't expect me to say that I miss you. That's what lovers do. We are married.
- Two people living together is enough noise. Let's not over-communicate.
- And please, no surprises. I hate it.

I think I was still getting used to the idea of marriage when I became a mother. Once my fertility was registered, and I begat a child, my points in the family grew exponentially. An uncle who I hadn't spoken to in ages sent me an e-greeting. Another one wanted to add me as a friend on Facebook. Cousins who had been procreationally active got in touch and offered their two bits. My family finally loved me!

Clearly, marriage was an aberration for me, but motherhood was not. It was something I seemed to find factory settings for quite easily; it was also something I could do with the kind of consistency I never thought I had. I couldn't do the same for wifehood. Or maybe I couldn't last long enough with the motions. I can't place a finger at what exactly went wrong, but I think at some point, I kept raising the bar for my husband and getting tired of playing the candy floss family and factoring everyone in. Especially the people I didn't really care about.

In a strange sequence of events, the man I married came up for scrutiny by me every single day after we made a baby together. It was something that crept into my head in an insidious way after I read one of his posts on Facebook which said something like "Interesting how most of marriage is spent plotting how not to get screamed at by the wife." This needs damage control, I thought. It was true. After the child, everything that he used to do semi-okay was now wrong. In my overwhelming pursuit of being a good mother, I had clearly lost out on being the good wife. I realised what happened. I had raised the bar, and I hadn't told him. Things that were okay until then were suddenly not okay. Everything began to matter.

Marriage is complicated. It is also very populated. There are too many people in a marriage. His. Yours. Facebook. Twitter. His friends who don't like you. Your friends who like you too much. Random strangers looking for subtext in status updates. Singletons trying to find reasons not to marry. Married ones who find a sense of gratification in the fact that perhaps you are as messed up as they are.

Parenting, on the other hand, is lonely. The world is not interested in it; it's not great copy. It doesn't have the layered politics of marriage, neither the intrigue of bachelorhood. You bring a human being into the world and you do as much as you can to ensure it grows up into a good human being. You go through the motions. Motions that sometimes debilitate.

Until you have a child, you could be married for years and never compare the textures of your lives. Your childhood. Your attitude to money. Your relationship with friends and family. Your sense of space. Your boundaries.Your hurt.

The minute you become a parent, the differences become glaring. It's as though the clouds that coalesced into a marriage now want to take their own shape and drift apart – because we think being a parent is more important than being a spouse. And there are questions that never accosted us earlier. There is the ominous responsibility of a whole human being's upbringing. A desire to fill in the details, to write it in a way that works for you.

A lot of marriage is autopilot. Plate his food. Remind him to eat. Remind him not to drink too much. Remind him to sleep. Remind him to wake up. Remind him to turn the TV off. Remind him to not game too much. Manage his papers: passport, KYC, aadhar card, income tax, mutual fund investments. I am good with the rituals. But once I became a mother, they got tiring. Sometimes, the wife wanted to switch off. Because the mother couldn't. There were days when I felt alone in our togetherness, and there were times when I felt together even when I was alone.

With the child, I was the bad cop, he was the softie. I was about boundaries. To him, love had no boundaries.

Poor men! One day they are the sperm, and the next day they are the parent who knows zilch about parenting. At least, women have the hormones that make motherhood a little more organic than it's purported to be. Men are so overwhelmed by the complexity of post-partum behaviour that the only thing they are looking for is a place to hide.

Since most of us didn't marry with checklists and did it for larger causes like love and hormones, it might be a tad shocking that the product of our conjugation is very often greater than the sum of our parts. I think if we have rigid ideas about how we should raise our children (bathing and brushing is sacrosanct, eating junk is sacrilege) we should have these conversations before our libidos get into a blur and the baby is already made.

Our relationship was full of notes – little post-its dripping with love to remind us of the way we were – on the microwave, on the fridge, on the TV screen, on the bathroom mirror. They are all locked in a little transparent pouch in my bookshelf. I keep looking at them and sighing wistfully. One day, the notes stopped. Must write more notes, I thought. But I had been sleep-deprived for four years by then.

'Husband' and 'wife' are big words. They come with tags and job-profiles attached. Role models to live up to. Social images to display. But our parents never told us what went into bringing up children or how children change the dynamic of a marriage. The questions seem banal: How much TV? How much chocolate? How many toys? How important is it to read? But in the answers lies an insidious divide. A 'his way' and a 'her way'.

So every time I felt I was losing my grip in the early years of our marriage, I would stare at the wall at a blown-up canvas print of us, obviously saturated with mirth. It could have been the moment. Whatever it was, it made me believe in 'we'. The sad thing is, it no longer does. Maybe there has been too much water under the bridge. Maybe I just want the rest of my life to begin. Maybe my default setting is 'single'. Maybe I am just tired of constantly factoring things and people. May be there is only so much lather-rinse-repeat I can do. In the motions of parenting, there was no time to fix 'us'. We drifted apart. One day, it was too late. And I didn't want to fix it any more.

A millennial friend recently said, 'Single is the new married' with a degree of nonchalance that I envy about millennials. It made me feel relieved. Although it is still hard to talk about my marriage in the past tense. May be I will get used to this too.

# 13. Home is where the cats are

I live in Bombay.

It was Bombay when I was growing up. It was Bombay when my mother gave me the keys to our home and said I was now old enough to let myself in after school (I was 10). It was Bombay when I first visited South Bombay and saw that people boarding taxis looked quite posh and that Bombay was as sexy as they made it appear in the movies. It was Bombay when I had my first kiss, the first time a man (other than my father) cooked for me, my first heartbreak, the first time I dumped someone.

It was Bombay when the glass window at my work desk at my first job reverberated. We were told there was an explosion at the Express Towers next door.

In a few months, it became Mumbai.

But whenever I am filling a form, I still find myself writing 'Bombay' I guess it will always be Bombay to me. I still look for the things that were rather than the things that are. I have that thing with my city. I am fiercely defensive about it. The longest I have ever lived away from it was when I went to teach English for a year in a school on a hill called Tiwai. It made me feel better that it wasn't another city, so technically, I wasn't cheating on Bombay. When I returned, although it was just a year later, my city seemed to have changed its configuration. Maybe it was me too. I didn't feel at home anymore like I used to.

I have moved nearly 20 homes since my childhood. In my marriage alone, I moved homes four times. I think every time you move, you raise the bar of a relationship. Moving house is a great way to measure your thresholds for each other, to test each other's adversity barometer. It is stressful to fit your life in boxes and then painstakingly set it up all over again only to take it apart a few years later. In a marriage, it helps you figure out how much of him and how much of you do you really want in a space that is 'us'.

Moving is also a great way to reinvent space. And since part of that space has you in the continuum, it means reinventing you. We have always rented, and no place was home for more than two years, and change in pin code was a rite of passage. Although ironically, the flat we clocked over two years in, was where my marriage finally fell apart.

A new flat is like a new relationship. There is a level of familiarity, and yes, there is love, but there is also intrigue. Nooks and crevices you haven't explored. Surfaces you haven't touched. Parts you haven't felt or smelt. Sometimes a house feels like home because of mosaic. Or imperfect walls, friendly nooks, a bookshelf just where you need it, a random hook on the wall, a hallway full of surprises, alcoves full of mystery, old-fashioned geysers, naked pipes and wires, book cases laden with World Books (an inheritance that a landlady once forced on me).

Suddenly, you could be kissing the evening sun instead of the sharp morning one. Or gazing at a mango tree instead of a concrete jungle. Or taking the stairs instead of a posh elevator that talks to you.

There are other benefits of moving:

- Sorting files, clothes, books, letters, mementos, photos, that you always meant to, but never did.
- You finally don't have to deal with people, noises, creatures who came as a package deal with your ex-apartment.
- Redefining your space. Claiming a corner that's all yours, a shelf, a cupboard, a balcony, a view.

My father's dodgy financial status and his pipe projects (which he always abandoned) ensured we were constantly moving house through my childhood. I was 18 by the time we had something close to a permanent home address. Even that didn't last more than six years. When I think of my childhood home, so many images spring to mind. My mother never kept any of our books and diaries as we never knew where we would move to next. I mourned the loss of *Black Beauty* and other books from my childhood for the first time when my son was born.

The words 'permanent home address' which appeared in almost every form you filled – whether it was a bank, a visa, your tax papers, a mobile connection, a job interview – made me nervous. I never knew what I was rooted to. There was no job or man that made me feel 'happily ever after'. My pen always hovered around those ominous blanks, not knowing quite what to fill. The only thing permanent in my life was my parents. I promptly directed all enquires of permanence to them, and filled in their address.

My friends often said I had the knack of turning any place into a home, even my hostel room that I inhabited for three years. I had a trunk that travelled with me everywhere; it was full of knick knacks, artefacts, lamps, and other things that I was collecting for my real home. It didn't take me long to turn a room or a space into home. A lamp here, some cushions there, happy curtains, some art on the wall, and every place I inhabited (and there have been far too many) became home effortlessly. They all had their issues, but each one had redeeming qualities that made them dependable. The work I put into spaces somehow was infinitely more rewarding (and less depleting) than the work I put into men. Sometimes, they made me run; at other times, I couldn't make them stay. I wish I could give myself as totally to the people I love as I do to the places I inhabit. Moving home – that thing which makes many people queasy, unsettled, anxious – was always the most natural thing for me. I got attached to places and apartments but never enough to miss them. I think this survival instinct kicked in pretty early in my life. I found change to be my most reliable companion. My mother kept reminding me it was a sign I had to settle down. She meant marriage of course.

And then there were cats of course. Cats made their homes in our transient homes, they loved us unconditionally, they slept on our tummies, in the nooks of our arms, they gave birth on our ankles, we looked after their babies and one day they grew up and new cats found us. Cats have seen me through love, heartbreaks, moving homes, marriage and baby. If there was a strong memory of a house, there was sure to be a cat that went with it.

Through most of my twenties, when love was elusive, it was always an apartment that made me feel loved. Every time I got derailed, it was always four walls that reclaimed me, that hugged me back, no matter what. I had to agree, I was a homemaker in disguise.

Right from my twin-sharing pad in Bandra which is now an opulent high rise, to the little studio in Khar to the doll-house next to Lilavati hospital in Bandra with secret cupboards, secret ironing boards and not-so-secret views – I loved them and they always loved me back. Book cases, ironing boards, dining tables, kitchen shelves, a nook here, a tree there, a frond of a palm that actually broke into my window, disallowing me from ever shutting it, and allowing me to make friends with a squirrel as he lived in the halfway house between the tree and my home. Of course, the cats were back in my life.

I thought marriage meant home, or permanence – that be-all, end-all feeling of settling down, of casting anchor. It meant that one stopped running and stood still. And then one day, I gave birth and truly realised the meaning of standing still.

My Cancerian husband was always averse to change while the Gemini in me celebrated it (it came from my nomadic childhood, with my father having trained us to fit into any space within 24 hours). Before our impending moves, he spent days gazing at familiar piles of wires, controllers, chargers coated in dust and grime, sighing that it will not be the same anymore. It was clear we had totally different fixations.

I usually made a deal with him and used the new flat as an excuse to buy us something I knew meant a lot to him. So that it becomes a metaphor for happy change, rather than a melancholy one as is wont to be for someone like him who ordinarily starts flapping if I so much as move his futon by an inch. So he got his 42 inch LCD (and then 50, and 72), and I got to do up a house all over again.

In all the years I was married, the one place I always had the best dreams in was my mother's house. It was the one place I felt protected, nurtured, off-duty. It was the place that continued to feature as 'permanent home address' in all the documents that one needs to define one's residence in a country.

Ironically, around the time my marriage fell apart was when I won an allotment in the Government's subsidized housing scheme and I finally had a permanent home address, all my own. It was what rescued me, not because I had no place to stay or nowhere to go, but I really needed to belong to something and nurture it all over again. I was invested enough in a piece of real estate to get utility bills in my name. I was no longer a tenant, I was an owner. It doesn't change the way I belong to Bombay but it just makes the relationship more complicated. It was like being married all over again. I bought a tea pot, shower curtains, table mats. I painted my ceilings bright yellow and leaf green. I got fairy wall paper for my son's room. I was home. Every square inch of space here is chronicling my life – and my child's. Yes, the father is missing from the picture, but there is always someone or something missing, isn't there? They say art is in the negative space.

In the end, a home is like a marriage. You have to be invested in it for the long haul for it to all come together, make sense. I couldn't do marriage well, so my home is the closest thing I have to it. There was nothing magical or transformative about the apartment I ended up buying. It didn't have the magical view of a park like my mother's house, nor did it have an amaltas tree in full bloom like my home on the hill. It didn't have sparrows visiting or cosy nooks and alcoves like my mosaic floored apartment. It didn't really smell of the ocean like my hostel room with rice paper lamps. But bit by bit, it came together. I always do the curtains first, and this time I chose black and white, although I am a colour person.

I feel a sense of belonging and rootedness all over again. I didn't realise real estate could have the effect on me that a person I loved couldn't. I don't flinch anymore when asked to fill my permanent home address and it's not because I own a few hundred square feet of real estate. It's because I finally feel I'm home, each time I walk into my apartment and draw open the drapes and find the exact same cookie cutter lives around me. Except the sun and moon have a different story to tell every day.

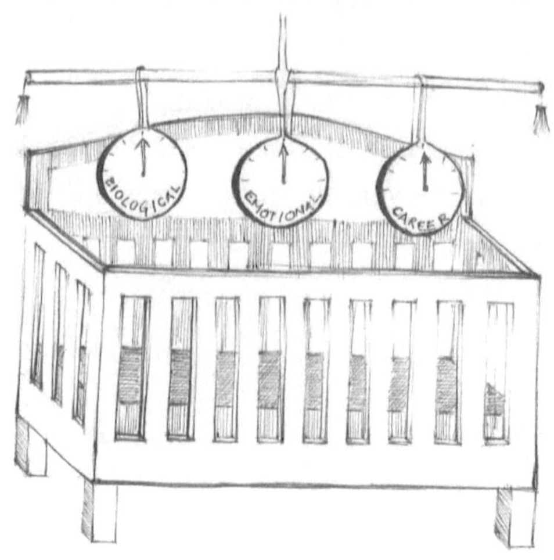


# 14. On having a child

When I was growing up, I thought I would get married by 27, because that's when I would find the perfect guy, would have settled in my dream job and aced it. I would have a baby at 30. And would swing back into my career by 35.

30 came and went, and I neither had the dream job nor the man. The baby of course had flown off the radar. My mother treated me like a time-bomb with every oncoming birthday although she was still the first person to wish me. Soon, relatives stopped asking me when I would settle down. Meanwhile, the rest of my friends were busy tying the knot and popping babies. I was busy playing the cool aunt and buying books that no one else would buy for them.

One day, I was 35. And I was told that I had totally missed the man and baby bus. I was a certified serial singleton while all my friends were making babies on loop. I was the cool aunty who gave the best gifts, treated babies like grownups and humoured mommies.

I could do all this, and go home, to my bed and get my nine hours of sleep. I didn't have to spoil it all by becoming a mom.

In the next five years, dream job, man and baby happened. I didn't plan it this way. But the fact that I had stopped thinking about them perhaps had something to do with it.

Was I ready? Hell no. Being a cat lady, playing aunt all those years, buying baby clothes, books and toys, playing peekaboo was hardly a qualification. I had no idea how one tiny person can change your life so irreversibly, enough for you to never be able to find factory settings again. I still go to bed wondering if I could, just for one day, wake up feeling single. And the strange part is, I have a good kid, and he is fun for the most part and I have no idea of the person I could be without him around. Does that mean I was ready for him? No.

My friend A's kid and mine share the same name. Hers is 18, mine is 8. She and I are the same age. Hmm, maybe it's a good thing to have kids early, I thought. You can just get on with the rest of your life soon. She has entered the second phase in her career, and pursuing her new entrepreneurial role with renewed vigor. We met last year. And then she told me about the black hole her life had been for the better part of the last 20 years. And then I felt bad that I was backpacking the countryside and switching boyfriends when she was tending to two kids, trying to get a new degree to stay relevant and managing a home.

When someone tells you what is the right time to have a baby, they are actually talking body time. Which is also fairly subjective, because your body is not readier just because it is younger neither is it less able because it is older. I never thought I would be able to dissect it this way, but there are three things in close competition in this whole phenomenon of baby-readiness: the biological clock, the career clock and the emotional clock.

For the purpose of convenience, let me divide this into three time zones when babies are usually had: the 20s, the 30s, the 40s. The inbetweeners get the worst deal. And ironically, this is the time when most women are choosing to have kids- the early thirties.

The flipside to this is: women who have their kids in their twenties actually have a shot at having their life back in their forties. On the contrary, women who have kids late have been there, done that, hopefully ticked off some items on their bucket list.

But no matter how much you factor in and how ready you are with a plan C, D and Z, a baby is one thing that will most certainly throw you off the loop and leave you wondering: is this what I bargained for? And worst, you will use your situation to feel that sense of entitlement because others did it to you and you will never forgive them.

Motherhood is the most irreversible thing that can ever happen to you. And yet it is the one thing that is the least thought through. Most women end up having babies either when it's too early for them to actually evaluate what's happening, or too late for them to have the luxury of thinking it through.

But I find the whole process of 'waiting until you're ready' to be a ridiculous idea, because it's based on the premise that one can actually 'prepare' for parenthood. It's a baby. It's as unpredictable as you are. My two bits on this: You are truly ready for a baby when you are truly ready for yourself. Because the extremes of who you are and what you can or cannot endure fully sink in post motherhood. And it is not always a happy place to visit, because you never know what you are going to find out. But if you really want to have a child, you are as ready as you will ever be.

I can't really tell you when you are ready for motherhood but I can take a good guess at when you are not:

1. You are not ready because you have a stable job you love: The job will be the most difficult thing to navigate post

baby, because it will always demand a rational side of you that will often run in short supply. Plus there will be more able, less-baggage workers dying to take your place when you are busy planning night feeds.

2. You are not ready because you have a willing partner: Once the sperm contribution has been made, most partners will run out the door and invent meetings and difficult work projects that keep them as far away from home as possible. If this is non-negotiable, you need to have that talk before you jump into sex on ovulation days.
3. You are not ready if you think having kids is fulfilling. You are better off winning medals at sport or cracking sales targets. There is nothing fulfilling about never knowing if you are good enough.
4. You are not ready if you think having a child will take your marriage to another level: On the contrary, this will be the most trying time of your marriage, but no one will tell you that because reproduction just means more companies can sell you more things for the rest of your life. And there is a lot of money to be made.
5. You are not ready because the child has two sets of grandparents intact: After the initial photo-ops, most grandparents are difficult to keep and involve emotional blackmail of the highest order.
6. You are not ready because all your friends have babies: There is no guarantee that their babies will be willing playdates. Or holiday companions.
7. You are not ready because you have had a cat. Make that several cats: Cats do not talk. Or whine. Or ask you to read the same book 29 times.
8. You are not ready because you were a really good baby sitter for your friends: There is always an exit plan for other people's kids. None for your own.

9. You are not ready because you like children: Children as playmates and amusement devices and children as things to care for 24x7x365 are very different things.
10. You are not ready because you have enough money: It is never enough. Remember the black hole?
11. You will never feel grown-up enough to know what to do, be a role model, give hope and direction to a small innocent child who will never tire of questions.
12. You are not ready just because you have a stable enough marriage.

I can say this with a certain amount of confidence that I am a better mother than I have ever been a daughter, sister, wife or friend. I have no clue how this happened and I do not believe age or hormones had anything to do with it.

Having a child was not the most strategic decision of my life. Nor was it the most emotional one. Having done it, I went through the motions. I am good with motions. Then my friends told me I was a natural as a mother and I wondered. Me? Natural? Yes, I did cats, and could fake excitement at baby photos or children's birthday parties. But that was about it. Unless you held me for the fact that I had become a mother to my mother during her open-heart surgeries. Did that really qualify me to have child?

In the loneliness of stay-at-home motherhood, the internet became my best friend. I began to read arguments and even research papers in favour of and against children. I could only think of it as a conspiracy theory. Why now, I thought. It's already done.

It is trendy these days to write about not having children, and there are many mornings when I wake up and wonder: had I really thought this through? May be not.

Maybe my reasons weren't deep enough. I never thought having a child would complete me, or for that matter, marriage would. I have never been afraid of being alone; in fact I usually crave it. I'm not generous enough to love unconditionally, nor have I been worried about being looked after when I'm old. It's unlikely that I will join the 'Parenting was the best thing I did with my life!' cult. No thank you. Well, once you have done it, it's like you don't want to admit you screwed up, so you may as well celebrate it.

I waited for that moment when holding a child in my arms would evaporate every other sadness in my life, but sorry to report, it didn't happen. Plus, I did cats, and it was way cooler to be a pet-parent. We can all lead exciting, chaotic lives, make love to our smart phones, travel, have recreational sex, backpack on a whim, live life to the fullest. Who wants kids?

So then, what was it?

Could it be about happiness? But the internet tells me that children rank lower in pleasure-giving than cooking, watching TV, exercising, talking on the phone, napping, shopping, or even housework ! (I was nodding through the list)

It's definitely not about bringing a couple closer. If marriage is fragile, children make a tsunami out of it. They take a small crack and turn it into a fissure of irreparable magnitude. They are a reminder of a life and a spontaneity that was, they make us realise that the gap between our fantasies and our reality is huge.

For a lot of women it's about getting something right. If not the man, the baby. Haven't you noticed that people who actually end up with their soul-mates take much longer to make the babies?

Yes, children do the most unexpected, kind, and loving things that send a rush of hormones to your brain. Or whatever it takes to feel good. Like my four-year old Re built me a house with his blocks. Or massaged my stomach when I said I had a tummy ache. Or shouted at a taxi for trying to overtake me.

Then there are gentle kisses. Cheeks to bite. Baby breath. It's addictive.

Yes, the moments of joy are pure and unparalleled. But so are the moments of frustration, despair and anxiety.

We have too much time to be grown-up, too little to be children. We have forgotten how to laugh, cry, jump in abandon, sing and dance at whim, eat, play, love without an agenda. We are all hiding behind our adult masks, pretending to be all grown-up. It's exhausting, this grownupness. Etiquette, protocol, political correctness – they are all collectively conspiring to render us clones of each other.

Children ask questions, don't take no for an answer, don't say 'yes' too easily and almost say nothing to please. Spending time with a child keeps your dissent alive. It makes you question authority, it makes you wonder why you do what you do, it makes you happy, sad, angry, curious. Some of us hold on to the child in us, others let go. But in the end, it is the child in us that sets us free, no matter what we choose to do.

Every year, on my son's birthday, we sit together and watch videos of the past few years. It feels gratifying and so much fun, although it did feel like tedium at the time.

But I think what I like the most about having a child is that every once in a while, I get to see the world without a lens.

Because I want to believe that if the moon does not 'follow' us when we drive back home from the park, it can actually lose its way.

Because I want to believe that every watermelon has mamma slices, dada slices and baby slices.

Because I want to wake up when it's sun o'clock.

Because I liked that part of me that is less impatient and self-involved than the me that was.

Because I was the kind of person who was likelier to regret the things I hadn't done than the things I had.

Because sometimes, you need to slow down. And that's what a child does to you. But innately, you should want to.

One of the side-effects of having Re is that he has brought me closer to my inner child. And so I feel grateful to him for teaching me these little things:

To laugh. Always. With abandon. Like you really mean it. As loud as you can. It's good for your lungs. And it really makes your face come alive. Know anyone who doesn't look good laughing?

To sing. Loudly. Or even softly. Whistle. Sway along. Sing like the world belongs to you. It will.

To dance. Anywhere, to anything. Dance like you know no fear, no inhibitions. Like your body is your best friend. Dance when no one expects you to.

To hug. Because no matter how big or small you are, you always feel happier after a hug.

To clap. Because it makes a nice sound. And when you are happy and you know it, you must clap your hands. The song says so.

To cuddle and kiss. Because everyone has to know they are loved.

To ask questions. Because it is important to know. Everything.

To cry. Because sometimes it is important to let people know that you are upset. Also, it always guarantees a cuddle.

# 15. In-lawfully yours

When I was a little girl, I would often come home from play to find my mother weeping, her eyes all red, and she would pretend she had been chopping onions or some such. I would then walk into the other room to find my grandmother (my mother's mother-in-law) and my aunt (her sister-in-law) whispering while munching on the eats with their evening coffee. It didn't take me long to realise my mother's tears was courtesy something they said to her. Later that night, I would also notice that my parents didn't speak to each other. I saw that whenever my parents fought, the fights that involved defending each other's people resulted in the longest sulks. My dad seemed to go about his life quicker than my mother. She was the one pretending to chop onions for a long time, even though there was no evidence of onions in the food we ate.

Somehow that visual got imprinted on my mind and I thought of marriage as something that divided the world into

HER people and HIS people. Post my mother's in-law saga, I had actually made up my mind that I would marry an orphan so I would never have to deal with in-laws. It didn't quite turn out that way though.

Marriage is a chance to acquire a new family, they say. For better or worse, this is a family that hasn't shared the same backstories as you, didn't know you as a child, didn't know your moods, quirks, what makes you happy, sad, angry, quiet. So, unless you marry your childhood sweetheart or the boy next door, there is no telling what you are really getting into. For some reason, the term in-laws conjures up visions of people we are legally bound to like (despite having no history with them). If the word in-law is in the name, the relationship is bound to be tricky. If they had called it something else, perhaps we wouldn't have been so wary of it. I wonder why husbands and wives don't carry the tag.

Unlike your parents or siblings who you can often be rude with, stop talking to for long periods of time, or do things without offering an explanation, decorum is the key in the in-law vocabulary. So is consistency. Now you know why friends are the best thing to have?

When newly married, most of us, however fleetingly, do the in-law dance: this is a series of meaningless, often ridiculous motions you go through to please those related by blood to that special person you have exchanged vital body fluids with. The tricky part is that the in-laws want you to keep adding new moves to the dance, or do it with more intensity and frequency. This includes saying pleasant things about how they look or what they are wearing for the most part, wishing them on anniversaries, birthdays and whatnot in person, via email/text, and on all social media platforms they are on (preferably tagging all others in the family who are on it too). I call it the pleasing the in-law phase and I have no idea why women do it unless they have to live with their in-laws, which seems quite rare these days. I thought I could do it for a year or two and then phase off, but I was wrong. Remember here that if you wished a certain-in-law on her anniversary, bought her gifts on her birthday, you will have to keep doing it on loop for as long as she (or the marriage) lasts.

The problem with this dance is: you can't stop. There is no end point, no finite time period beyond which they cease to matter. If you have children, they matter in a whole new way. Women who do the in-law dance to make things genial in their marriage at the start, often find that it's a trap they can never extricate from. Because new members keep getting added to this dance: other in-laws, children, spouses, newly manufactured relatives, old relatives repackaged and repurposed ... it never ends. I often saw friends being treated as the beck-and-call girl by their in-laws when they showed a modicum of responsibility or initiative in one instance and I vowed that I will never go down that lane. Although I did act as chief cross country courier for a while for a sister-in-law and I was either delivering or picking up parcels, which made me feel like I worked for DHL.

Doing the in-law dance includes, but is not limited to – factoring them in for everything, smiling till your jawbones hurt, even though you want to grit your teeth at a sister-in-law who thinks two idlis is too much food, or another who avoids a family lunch at your parents' home because she was getting a Redbull vending machine installed at hers.

But I smiled and waved for the photo-ops.

Until I realised it was always about the photo-ops. There were never any real conversations, no lunches and dinners around a table laden with food, no afternoon snoozes, no family travels and misadventures therein. We had to RSVP to all weddings, even in the immediate family – that is how formal it was. And once social media took off, all communication was on timelines.

There are types and types of in-laws and they range from the over-sharers to the overly-sensitive to the control freaks to the strings-always-attached to the no-boundaries variety. Each one involves careful, unique, and often hair-splitting negotiations. It doesn't really help if they are geographically far away. In-laws have this knack of getting under your skin remotely and technology has made it easier for them to do so. All you need is a tag really.

There are two questions you need to ask yourself before you decide what your in-law strategy is going to be (and think these through clearly, for you cannot change a strategy once adopted, unless you change the husband)

Have you set boundaries?

What are your expectations?

A crucial decision to take early on in your marriage (particularly in these times) is whether you want in-laws on your social media. I never gave it much thought earlier, but I am beginning to realise I am not comfortable with the coexistence of friends, acquaintances, school and college mates, work colleagues, family and in-laws in one space. Thankfully, my family was easiest to 'unfriend' as they didn't really care or notice either way. But as I went about pruning my list, no prizes for guessing who it did not go down well with at all. My advice on social media would be: don't have anyone on it that would have a problem being off it at some point.

A search for 'in-laws' on google reveals endless pages on the mother-in-law – a person I reckon everyone loves to hate (chiefly because she is a consistently significant 'other' woman in your husband's life before you came along). The poor thing bears the brunt of all the negativity directed at in-laws. Surprisingly there is little on fathers-in-law, brothers and sisters in law and other species. Mother-in-law seems like a collective noun for all in-laws and often gets the rap, but there are plenty of fish in the sea that are in equally contentious zones.

The thing about marriage is: years later, you are still figuring out this person you married and every day is a revelation. And then to top it all, there is social media now and you have to 'friend' and 'follow' not just him, but his entire extended family, comment and like photos with alacrity and flash emojis at them once in a while (this happens by autopilot to some). 'Liking' an in-law's social media post has now become as important as remembering their birthday (a thing which social media helps with immensely, and if you are not one of the first five people on their timeline that day, you are not really integrated into family. I guess I never made the cut).

So much work that managing your own family, who thankfully are miles away from social media feels like a breath of fresh air!

I think the basic problem with my marriage was SHOW vs TELL. My 'show' family had married into his 'tell' family. Also a no-hugs, no air-kisses family had married into PDA ambassadors. I still did a fair job of going through the motions for the first two years of my marriage, and then abruptly stopped, because, well, there was only so much of me to fake and plus there was a baby to manage now.

Okay, I know there are women out there who will go, 'Such a cliché! I absolutely laaarrrrrv my in-laws!'

Well, fuck you.

This chapter is for the huge majority who can't make sense of their in-laws but don't know how to say it (or can't, which is probably more common).

To come back to the mother-in-law: I have a feeling that beyond a point, men don't really know what to do with their mothers. For a very long time, they are in denial about this, as they are with most things, till one fine day, they meet a woman who can 'do mothers'. This is the point at which they are at first in shock and awe, and then eventually heave a jubilant sigh of relief, as if exclaiming, "Take her ... and do what you want with her. Amuse her, talk to her, listen (most important), call, write, bitch, gossip, whatever. But leave me out of it ... please."

And before you know it, you get outsourced your husband's entire family and he breaks free, just like it happened to me.

A huge mistake I made – and it was all my fault; I dug my own grave at my *sangeet* speech – proclaiming on stage that I now had two moms instead of one. So post marriage, I found myself compulsively communicating with two mothers – his was definitely more tech savvy than mine, so in a sense easier to do (or so I thought. I just had to flood her wall with emoticons, beam at random forwards, sometimes even take quizzes, and such). As for my mother, conversations were key, with talking and listening being of equal importance. Fumbling with either of the two would immediately get her antennae up, as would a slight inflection in my voice, which set her thinking, 'I wonder what's wrong and how I can fix it.' My mother believes in a strict two-way communication, so there is no way you can avoid a confrontation. May be that's why I have become quite good in that department.

In the early months of our marriage, I found myself diligently calling the mother-in-law and updating her on events of the week. It just absolved the husband of that one little ritual he used to perform. Soon, I became good at it, so much so that my best friend couldn't help observing how well I did the mother-in-law. I tried suggesting to her that I might actually have social skills or perhaps I was amiable, contrary to what she believed and she banished it instantly as rubbish. 'Now don't give me that ... you don't get along with seven out of ten people. Just admit, you are good at the stuff.'

She was wrong. I was far from having mastered political correctness. Because a simple phrase like 'Hold your horses' which you may have used innumerable times with your mother has a tsunami effect when used on your mother-in-law. More so, when it is used in context with a visit to her soon-to-be-born grandchild. I was 41 weeks pregnant, my hormones were raging, and the only people I could deal with (or wanted to) at the time were the mother and the husband (both of whom I could bark at unflinchingly and they would get it). My mother-in-law popped up in my inbox, announcing chirpily that she wanted to fly down instantly. I was afraid of her causing an imbalance in my tiny apartment with two cats (who she didn't particularly like) and a baby (which she was dying to like), thereby resulting in me not being able to be the beatific mom that I had intended on being (however dim the possibility). I unleashed a "Hold your horses. You can always come later when things are settled" and hit 'send'. And that was that. 'Hold your horses' became the single most evil thing in history that a daughter-in-law could ever say to a mother-in-law.

No one told me marriage was about so much nuance.

I realised that the difference between mothers and mothers-in-law is the difference between a cat and a dog – while one is discreet and invisible, the other is conspicuous and visible. Every action is announced, every thought is spoken, every silence filled. It takes work. Work that the husbands don't want to do. Also, I was a cat person. No matter how old you get, your mother will still be the person you can hang up on, walk out the door on, stop midsentence to call out her bullshit or just tell her to stop talking or whining. Do this with the mother-in-law and you become the 'evil-in-law', a tag I soon acquired. Once you have tried enough to make sense of his family, and they still don't, you might think that since you otherwise have such a good relationship with this man, you could perhaps tell him what you think. It's a dangerously slippery slope from there. Also, (and maybe I'm generalizing here) Indian men are peculiar when it comes to their people and I had no clue of this whatsoever. The day you start telling your husband exactly what you think of his mother is the beginning of the end of your marriage.

Now while it is totally okay to think your father is the greatest idiot on earth or that a certain aunt is conniving and manipulative, or a certain cousin is the worst kind of gossip monger – throwing some light on anything that casts aspersions on the hitherto flawless in-laws to your spouse is tantamount to marriage harakiri.

Which is why: what you think about your in-laws must stay with you until the day you die. The only people you can tell is your family. Because they will never rat on you. Even if they hate you.

Luckily I have no such issues now. I found me back. Well, it is a relief that I don't have to do the in-law dance or any form of dance any more. I am 48 now, it's time I start being me finally.

I regularly used fodder from my real life to write my columns week after week, until my mother pointed out she just has to read the newspaper to know what's going on in my life. I said I am a writer; everything is copy, in classic Nora Ephron style and my mother totally got it. I must admit, it was addictive. When some nuanced bits about in-law conversations found their way there, all hell broke loose. War was declared on social media and creative license completely subjugated. I then realised that what you say and who you are should always be separate things.

I put in a disclaimer in my blog: Anything you say can and will be used against you. (I guess I have got myself covered for this book).

I notice that my parents, after 50 years of marriage, finally have some really nice bonds with their respective in-laws (very often the in-laws having a better likelihood of having their back than their own people) and I smile. Perhaps if you ride the wave long enough, things do get better and more organic. But I do know that most of the work was done by my mother.

# 16. On raising a child

I think the term parenting was invented roughly around the time my child was born. And with that came words like tiger mom, camel mom, lamb mom and every-other-animal-except-human mom. I am happy to report that I am not aspiring for any of these positions. For now I'm happy to be called I-don't-give-a-shit-mom and smile beatifically when people are talking about parenting.

Okay I should know better; I wrote a parenting blog and column for years. I constantly wrote parenting scripts in my head. I was okay being daunted by my own fears and insecurities, not knowing if I was doing the right thing as a parent, but often resigning myself to 'this will do for now' and putting it out there. It's like people who write about finding love and have no clue how to do it for themselves. Somehow, writing about relationships wasn't as hard, because, in the end, all men and women fall into fixed matrices and it's not very hard to extrapolate and theorize. With children, it's trickier.

It's been nearly eight years of being a mother and I can't say I know things better now, or that they have become easier (as friends constantly promise you). In the past few years, I have made many virtual friends, some of who I even met in real life. I made a few enemies, like the lady who wrote to me saying I had no business bringing a child into this world without buying a house first. Or the one who thought I was being self-indulgent when I wrote about stay-at-home moms. Or one who wrote I had no business calling myself a single mom if it hadn't been established on paper.

It is ironic that for the toughest job in the world, there is no qualification or training required. We get to be parents just like that. For most of us, it is like being hit by a thundercloud. But no one wants to admit that they feel unprepared for parenthood, however much it makes you flounder. It is one of the best-kept secrets of any household. That is why we have pictures (and selfies) to remind ourselves of what we can be. Pictures are nice. Pictures tell stories. Sometimes they reveal subtexts that we didn't even know existed. In pictures, we look like a candy floss movie – integrated, art-directed, and full of joie de vivre.

Parenting is like being in the Big Boss house without even being aware that there are cameras in your child's head. That everything you say and do is being recorded. There is no editing, touch up or colour correction. You can strategise how you will present yourself at a date or an interview and make an impression, but as a parent, you are there, in the moment, in all your naked vulnerable state, without makeup or filters. There is no auto-correct, and children pick up on everything. Even the things you don't say.

But I am tired. I am tired of curating memories. I am tired of monitoring things I say (or don't say).

I am just happy that he goes to school every day, does stuff on his own and now can read too. I am happy to answer questions I know stuff about and unafraid if I am ignorant on certain things and need to catch up. I can't be it all and do it all.

And I know this: I am okay if my child shows me the way.

Here are a few things that I don't give a shit about:

**I don't care what he learns in school.** I chose the school only because it has a good arts programme and they teach the kids karate and songs about science and the environment. It was one thing I wouldn't have to do. Also I look at school as an extended form of daycare, so I am happy with the basics. The more I expect from it, the more I have to do. And I won't do THAT.

**I don't know the difference** between ICSE, CBSE, IG, IB, IGCSE or any new boards that may have been invented without my knowledge and frankly, I don't care. I don't think learning comes prefixed with labels. I am still learning although I may have some labels.

**I hate homework**. Okay let me correct that. I hate that I may have to help with homework. So I pretend it doesn't exist. My time with my kid is my time with my kid. It cannot be an extension of school time. I have enough trouble being a mother. I don't want to be a tutor. Besides I would suck at it. Having been a teacher doesn't help.

**I hate it when other moms** on Whatsapp discuss homework. I think they are all losers. I really do. I mean what kind of person would triple check what a child says is homework just in order to ascertain that it indeed is? Your kid knows what to do. It's just that you don't trust him/her. Losers.

**I am constantly nervous** that the child will come with a note in his almanac or some circular will be issued from the school that parents have to do a project/make some costume/prop. I don't want to be a part of it.

**I am really bored of listening** to people talking about their kids' achievements. Like slit-my-wrists bored. Do something yourself and tell me, for Christ's sake.

**I love it when my kid plays with dolls**, puts on makeup for them, paints shoes on them, does their hair, adds sequins to their clothes. If you have a problem with it, it's your problem.

**Sometimes I forget the difference** between my outside voice and my inside voice. My kid calls me shouty. But then it's okay, because he forgets it too. So we are even.

**I sometimes make feeble attempts** to ask him whether he would like to learn ballet, the piano, or tennis maybe, knowing fully well that I will have to sacrifice more hours of writing or doing what I want for it, but then he says no; he already knows ballet. And the piano. I don't argue. I am relieved and let him be.

I have often heard this (even among very aware parents): I don't know how to entertain my child. Or heard them whining when the more active partner is away that they are stuck with entertaining their child. I don't get this. Why is entertaining your child even a thing? Why is it a norm? I feel if one is teaching them that this is how life is – a series of fun-filled, action-packed time capsules on loop, where there is no time for recovery, stillness or nothingness – you are in a dangerous place. It's a slippery slope from there.

I got into this trap for a brief while when Re was still in his crib and had a limited geography within which to entertain himself (although my cats helped hugely). It was boring as shit for me. Singing. Making faces. Speaking in funny voices. Peekaboo. Yes, Re loved it. But then I realised I am not his playmate. Why should I pretend to be? As soon as he started crawling and then walking, he was on his own. And he found plenty to amuse himself with, mostly in the kitchen. I still have a video of him somewhere where he is trying to sort a bunch of cherry tomatoes and talking to himself. And one of him trying to roll a chapati with a rolling pin and board.

Every time the other parental unit arrives laden with games/ toys, I arch my eyebrows. Collaborative games get me worried because playing with my child is not something I really enjoy. I have boundaries. I don't play. On the few travel dates that I have had with fellow parents, I have always noticed that they come armed with suitcases full of toys, gadgets, books, games. And I say: but it's just two nights. Why do you need so much? And they reply: Oh, if we keep them entertained, we can get more time for ourselves.

From then, I started traveling alone with Re and it was much more satisfying.

Yes, we all want our children to have a happy childhood with a variety of experiences. We just have to stop curating it for them. I have seen friends plan reading lists for their kids, populate their schedules with every activity that looks good on paper and that they can tick off an imaginary list.

I feel like telling them: It's your life, not a pinterest board.

Yes it's important to attend to their needs, engage in fun and games with them, keep conversations going, but all this can be quite simple. But when you make it your mission that your kids are always entertained and having fun, it's like you are trying to tell them that this is how life ought to be. You are not allowing their imagination and creativity to come up with something on their own. Besides life is all about a lot of mundane things on loop and our kids need to know that and be a part of that too.

You are told you will lose a part of yourself when you become a mother. So you lose yourself. Then you are told you probably won't be able to do all the things you're used to doing. So you stop all the things you had fun doing, things that defined you, that made you You. You are told you will be transformed by this experience in ways you could never imagine and no one could ever accurately describe to you. You start looking for your halo. A few years later, you find there is none. It was never meant to be. And there are no motherhood rehabilitation centres. It's as though losing yourself was just a rite of passage to becoming a mother.

I knew motherhood wouldn't be easy, but I had no idea just how hard it would be. And sadly, the wisdom of motherhood doesn't came attached with a pair of ovaries. Most of us are still fumbling around, doing things by trial and error, because the books are rubbish anyway. What they call 'instinct' is things you figure out as you go along. Some of the changes were absolutely not okay with me but it was up to me to renegotiate my way back into the world.

I am still learning to do motherhood in moderation. There are days when I feel so much love for Re that I need little else. There are days when I miss the me I was so much that I feel the need to reclaim her.

I used to be a get up and go woman. I quit jobs, I found jobs. I quit careers, I found careers. I quit men, I found men. I always went travelling in between. Sometimes I even travelled alone.

When women say motherhood changed them, the danger is that sometimes the change makes them unrecognizable. Few mothers have the time and self-love to indulge in contemplations of selfhood. Most days they play a false version of their true depleted self, keeping others at a distance, saying only what is expected from a mother: "I'm so thrilled, it's so amazing, such an incredible journey, I'm loving every second of it." I did it too. I did the blissed out new mother dance for a while, while a little bit of my selfhood got obliterated. Fortunately I was totally and completely aware of it when it was happening. I realised motherhood couldn't complete me. Only I could. No, even the all-encompassing love for my child never made me lose sight of the woman I was.

I am also unafraid in mother-love. I don't worry over Re growing into a teen, a man, having to make choices and mistakes. There will be confusion, anger, sorrow. He will fall in love. There will be heartbreaks. I just don't have to mourn them yet.

Now, after eight years of making difficult choices, negotiating day in and day out, there is still a lot left of me. I am raring to go, write more books, write fiction, write for children, do new things with my life, travel, teach, perhaps even study. Mother-love was not enough for me to feel me. I needed more, and I went after it. That was the only way I could retain my selfhood. That's the only way I want Re to remember me when I'm gone. Not someone who lost herself in him.

I realised my child deserves the fuller, happier version of his mother. The writer. The feminist. The traveller. I was constantly rearranging my life so that the self-respecting feminist, the loving mother and the ambitious writer could coexist. It was hard. It still is.

# 17. Things I think about more now

A few days back, a lady at the park said to me, "I love your haircut. It makes your salt and pepper come alive. So chic you look!"

We were walking in circles in opposite directions and had passed each other thrice before she decided to accost me and let me know. I was caught off guard. It was not my best hair day, plus I was sweating profusely and had slid bob-pins into my hair to keep them from my face.

I don't know why, but I found myself telling her how I once had cascading, curly, black hair and how I had a huge maintenance and greying issue post baby and kept snipping bits of it and eventually settled on a pixie.

"Ah, but I didn't see it then. I am seeing you now. You are gorgeous."

I have to learn how to take a compliment.

I will turn 49 this year. I am learning to remind myself that my gorgeousness is not past tense. That even with my greys, my pixie, the lines on my face, my threatening double chin, the blemishes on my skin, the lack of a waist, I am still enough. I have to believe in my hotness.

The lady at the parlour has finally tired of telling me to do facials, color my hair, do something about my blemishes, my permanent tan. My face and its imperfections don't bother me anymore. I feel good on most days and I have a bounce in my step. Thanks to EFT, I have learned to say 'I love you' to myself too. It's important they say, this self-love. From practice, I can say that it helps.

I spent most of my twenties thinking I was average. It was my thirties that helped me celebrate my uniqueness – my dusky skin, curly hair and unconventional face. My body also came into its own then, and I experimented a lot with clothes and hair. In my forties, I feel unabashedly hot. I find it weird when women are constantly apologizing for their bodies and figures and saying things like they have to lose more weight to be able to wear dresses or shorts or whatever. Men never seem to have those issues.

I have some rich, beautiful friends who often invite me to their parties where I meet more rich, beautiful people wearing clothes they will never repeat. As they clink their glasses and take selfies of themselves in their sunnies and pouts, they often discuss vampire facials, keto diets, their new workouts with their instructor, planking, scuba diving and chanting. It is not my business what people do with their face and body and how they live their life. I am just happy if it's joyful and creative and if it makes them happy.

Most of my friends have lost at least one parent; some have lost both. Some have kids, some don't; some have stayed married, others have not, some are single and happy being so. I reach out to every friend who has an ailing parent, asking them what I can do. I may give a miss to weddings, but I never forget condolences.

Even though I don't particularly like group chats I find myself telling my siblings over our endless family whatsapp chats that we should bury the past, have more family reunions, go back to the space we were as children. They seem to agree, but nobody makes any moves.

I still lose my cool with my parents, but I immediately want to make it right. I call my father. I never used to call my father; it was always my mother. I want my parents to do a nice world trip together before it's too late. What do you mean too late, snaps my brother. You know they don't have much time left, I tell him. What are you saying? They are only in their seventies.

I call my uncle in Coimbatore, my aunt in Baroda, I get my son to send voice messages to his paternal grandfather in Delhi, because they really soothe him. I never miss an opportunity to have a real conversation. I am not satiated by liking posts on social media.

I feel braver talking to my parents about death. I keep asking them if there is something they want to do or want done? I talk to them about their wills. My mother brushes it off saying all she wants is to go quickly, and to not spend endless days in hospital. My father laughs and says he's led a full life and will be happy to go on the field, where he is currently spending his life, growing things. My brother and sister don't want to talk about death. I know it's harder for them; they live on foreign shores and most likely won't be there when it happens. I will be the one calling them. I keep thinking about that call in my head.

My son, who is just about eight also asks me about death. We lost a cat a few years ago, and I have had conversations about death with him. He knows his grandparents won't live for long (there is a term for it: grandparent deficit. I read it in Time magazine. It's a term for how children these days have lesser grandparent time as people are marrying late and having children late, so the window keeps getting smaller).

I used to freak out about being single in my twenties; now I am just grateful I am not in the wrong relationship. I find being alone very calming for the most part. Yes, there are still butterflies in my stomach when I meet someone half interesting; yes, my heart is still not as robust as I thought it would be, but I find more things to do, better ways to move on.

When I left my husband, people asked me, "What if you never find love again?"

May be I won't. I knew it was a risk I was taking. I know it's a big reason for women to never leave their husbands. Added of course to the financial aspect of it, because let's face it, men still like to look at themselves as providers. And it's easier to be in a marriage than out of it.

But I don't feel alone anymore.

The loneliest thing is lying next to a person in bed and feeling no connection with him. I feel un-alone. I feel like I have finally found the space to be who I am. It just took really long. It's not a lonely place to be.

My favorite part of the day is still early mornings, when no one else is awake (except the cats) and I can be truly alone with my thoughts. It doesn't last very long, but it is the one thing that makes me look forward to going to bed at night.

I think the one thing we need to do more is constantly reevaluate our relationships. When we don't do that, they erode, they reach a point of stasis; they stop nurturing the self and the other person.

My mother is still the first to wish me on my birthday, although these days, my son tries to beat her to it. I still like my birthdays quiet although now I know too many people and thanks to social media, my birthday is also in the public domain. I miss my childhood days when my birthdays, in the blazing heat of May, were only about my family (perhaps an aunt or two who remembered) where my mother baked the cake and stitched my dress. As far as my school was concerned, I never had birthdays; everyone was away and no one wished me, although at the time I was relieved I didn't have to entertain anyone. These days, I am torn between going all out or just curling up at home with my family and cats. Last year I did something out of character and threw a birthday bash for myself at the Press Club, inviting all my friends. I figured I would never see them all in one place, given how times have changed, so this was my way of marking attendance (the last time I saw so many friends in one place was my wedding). There were over 30 of them. I might have a big bash when I'm 50, although I am tempted to hide in the hills again. Let's see.

I am taking more chances with my writing. With my child who is at a delicious age, I feel this purity of connection that often takes me to a less cluttered version of me. Sometimes I meet people I feel the same purity of connection with. It lifts me up, even if it is for a short while. I have this infinite capacity to nurture myself and constantly find ways of doing so.

I look back fondly at the times when there was only one of me to manage. She had friends she could see whenever she liked, and she didn't have to like multiple pages and things to show she liked them. The only handles she had belonged to her mugs and teapots. When her friends were upset with her, she knew because they told her so. She knew things before facebook or her timeline reminded her because she was good with dates and numbers. She didn't have to be 'liked' to be liked. She didn't have to keep track of her various avatars and ensure they are consistent. Her life was interesting even when she didn't curate it.

I think about myself when I am my mother's age often. I am not relying on my son to look after me, although I find myself asking him often; I don't know why. He says he will, and then he kisses me gently on my cheek and I feel all is well with the world – his and mine. I keep talking to like-minded friends about a halfway house for when we are 60. Okay 70. Where we can cease to be daughters, sisters, mothers, wives, and just be ourselves. Where we can all chip in, live, cook and love together, where we can leave behind our baggage of the past and just take off from where we left off. Where we can nurture each other, write, paint, sing, dance, grow things and make art. I am constantly plotting on where this place will me. Rishikesh. Goa. Himachal. I have a few ideas and I have four friends on this list already. I think I can make it happen.

## Afterthoughts

☞ Life is what happens between facebook posts.

☞ Never buy a dress you hope you can fit into. Never marry a man you hope you can change.

☞ As you grow older, you will fart from strange places.

☞ Call your father. He's the bloke no one calls.

☞ Don't trust a man who says he had 84 girlfriends.

☞ Learn to say 'Fuck you'. It's useful sometimes.

☞ You are never the first woman a man wanted to marry.

☞ Have a plan for when you are sixty that doesn't involve kids or a spouse. You may still have them, but have the plan anyway.

☞ There is no such thing as too much travel.

☞ Avoid thongs.

☞ Take backups. Everything crashes.

☞ Print photos. I know the future is digital, but you will thank me one day.

☞ There is no real reason to stay in touch with everyone in your family.

☞ If you have kids, try and get your kids to be friends with your friends' kids. It's better than trying to be friends with his friends' parents.

☞ Always stay groomed. You never know who you will run into and when.

☞ Most people talk because they are uncomfortable with silences, not because they have something useful to say.

☞ Take a gap year.

- ☞ If it's too much effort not thinking about a person, you are thinking of them too much.
- ☞ Make paper boats.
- ☞ There are people who make plans and there are people who show up.
- ☞ Try and find people you can be your pure self with. Never let go of them.
- ☞ Smile when you look at the mirror.
- ☞ Try living with an animal at least once in your lifetime.
- ☞ Cook. Feed.
- ☞ Never miss an opportunity to dress up.
- ☞ Make mistakes. Life will autocorrect.
- ☞ Sunscreen is overrated.
- ☞ Sometimes it's the choices you make. Sometimes it's the choices you didn't make. Either way, it's your life.
- ☞ Life is full of unfinished conversations. Try and finish them when you can.
- ☞ Don't try and understand social media etiquette. Read a book instead.
- ☞ Be.
- ☞ Do less.
- ☞ Lose control.

# Acknowledgements

I would like to express my deep gratitude and say a quick thank you to the following:

My cats, for occasionally getting off the mouse so I that I could write.

Abira, Sai, Nikita, Natasha for reading bits of the manuscript and telling me when too much was too much, or jumping in glee when I wrote something that touched you.

Every shampoo and conditioner who ever inhabited my life (if you are the type who reads acknowledgements before you read the book, this will be hard to decode)

Re for getting it that his mom is happiest when writing.

Amma for being mistress of the kitchen and providing me meals while I wrote, even though she would rather discuss "what sambar to make today?".

Aditi and Gul for your generous blurbs.

Geetu for getting the spunk of the book and visualizing a lovely cover. Kaavya, for transforming every chapter with your wild and imaginative drawings.

Everyone who is visibly or invisibly in the book.

And above all, Himanjali. I am so happy I found you. You are the most fun editor I have ever had. May our books live happily ever after.

Thank you all.

www.ingramcontent.com/pod-product-compliance
Ingram Content Group UK Ltd.
Pitfield, Milton Keynes, MK11 3LW, UK
UKHW041445070726
13610UKWH00009B/17